Praise for *The Bomb Cloud*

T0285495

Building out — as if in staggered waves — from a 'classified' photo in a family album, *The Bomb Cloud* grapples with the vexing indeterminacy that afflicts events that become history. What was her grandfather's role at White Sands, at Hiroshima? What took place in the realm of the unsaid? Doggedly forensic, self-scouring, Tyler Mills works the evidence and asks the hardest questions. There is a palpable tremor at the heart of her account.

Sven Birkerts, author of *Changing the Subject: Art and Attention in the Internet Age*

Tyler Mills is a gorgeous, deft writer, and to read *The Bomb Cloud* is to be seduced by a beauty which belies its content, like the children who played in the snow-like fallout of an atomic bomb test in 1940s New Mexico. Mills is also tenacious and truth-seeking, and *The Bomb Cloud* is an unflinching look at the horrors of atomic warfare on people, the environment, a nation's sense of self, and the repercussions, big and small, of faulty collective and personal memory, and of living inside a white supremacist patriarchy. "I had stepped into the murky stillness of the system that had put men in charge," Mills writes, "and I mucked up the dirt." Reading *The Bomb Cloud* will leave you feeling grateful for the muck.

Lynn Melnick, author of *I've Had to Think Up a Way to Survive: On Truma, Persistence, and Dolly Parton*

Mills writes that "the beauty of New Mexico is one of high contrast," and I feel that in this work as she tries to uncover unsettling truths with the lush language of a dexterous poet. In this powerful memoir that "brings disparate materials together [to] ... invite readers to look more deeply at them," she has "jigsawed the past together" through "study[ing] the shadows." A book of history, family, art, and legacy, *The Bomb Cloud* is as much about destruction and loss as it is about creation. Through lyric prose, photographs, and collage, Mills demonstrates for us the recursive nature of building a narrative map of the unknowable as she strives to reconcile what we know and what we've been told with what the records show.

Chet'la Sebree, author of *Field Study* and *Mistress*

Tyler Mills is a hauntingly powerful writer. Her new book, *The Bomb Cloud,* has levels of amazement that get richer the deeper you go. It's gorgeous stuff that you won't soon forget.

Luis Urrea, author of *The Devil's Highway*

The Bomb Cloud

The Bomb Cloud Tyler Mills

UNBOUND EDITION PRESS

Atlanta

FIRST EDITION

Printed in the United States of America

LIBRARY OF CONGRESS RECORD

Name: Mills, Tyler, 1983 — author.
Title: The Bomb Cloud / Tyler Mills.
Edition: First edition.
Published: Atlanta : Unbound Edition Press, 2024.

LCCN: 2023947690
LCCN Permalink: https://lccn.loc.gov/2023947690
ISBN: 979-8-9892333-0-4 (fine softcover)

Designed by Eleanor Safe and Joseph Floresca
Printed by Bookmobile, Minneapolis, MN
Distributed by Itasca Books

123456789

Unbound Edition Press
1270 Caroline Street, Suite D120
Box 448
Atlanta, GA 30307

PERMANENT

For G.S.M and D.M.

How then does light return to the
world after the eclipse of the sun?
Miraculously. Frailly. In thin stripes.
It hangs like a glass cage.

VIRGINIA WOOLF

Contents

I.

IV.

Coda

The Bomb
Cloud

I.

A Silent Film

[Pan of the White Sands Missile Range]

[No sound]

[Men walk around the scaffolding]

[The sky New Mexico blue]

[The bomb is set down by a crane]

[Some saucer-shaped clouds overhead]

[I miss the announcer's voice]

[A man begins climbing a ladder, but the film cuts out]

[The bomb looks like a larger *Star Wars* droid]

[It could carry instruments into the sea]

[I wish I could hear the men talking about it]

[Their lips move]

[One man rests his knee on the shell]

[A hook keeps it upright for now]

[They set a canvas tent around it, everything white inside]

[Now we're farther away]

[The men start walking away]

[The ones still there touch it with bare hands]

[The crane hoists it up the tower like the New Year's Eve Ball dropping in reverse]

[What would the announcer say now]

[Or now]

[It goes skyward]

[Brown screen]

[White screen]

[Brick-red screen]

[More happened, but I watched]

Wait. It's played again.

[Half a man's face burns for a second]

[It fists the air as it moves]

[What would the announcer say now]

[Or now]

Again. Play it backwards to the beginning.

[Red] [White] [A marshmallow blackening]

[Cut]

This Video Has Been Sanitized

US Department of Energy

Prologue

The first time I have seen a torii gate — the tree trunk poles, the slightly concave roof — was at the Botanic Garden in the unceded homeland of the Lenape people. In the garden that quiet, humid morning, I listened for the hum of traffic that usually carries its quick and cacophonous voice along Washington Avenue and Flatbush. Instead, the streets were nearly silent. Our cloth masks pressed pink and white flowers, blue and black paisleys, to our lips in the hazy air. We hardly saw anyone among the hedges and trellises, and when we did, we backed away nervously. Even being outside in a public place like this felt like breaking a rule. Birdsong filled the trees, and I stopped with my spouse and toddler to admire little yellow flowers.

I'd moved to Brooklyn from New Mexico a few months before the pandemic, so this was my first time at the Botanic Garden. I've never been to Japan, and I don't recall seeing a torii gate in person in any gardens I might have visited as a child or young adult. That August morning, the garden sunny and empty, was one of the first times the public could re-enter this beloved place during the first summer of the pandemic. The Brooklyn Botanic Garden officially re-opened at limited capacity on August 7, 2020, a day after the seventy-fifth anniversary of the US bombing of Hiroshima.

Somewhere, I wrote down the names of the starlike growths in the green. My toddler stopped to pick up sweet gum seed pods — spiny little worlds slightly smaller than golf balls. And then we rounded a corner. There we saw the wooden Shinto gate, reddish orange, standing at the edge of the pond. The structure reflected itself, stretching into the pond and up into the sky, extending in two directions. Upward and downward. This world and its mirror. We wound our way up the path, leaving the stroller at the bottom of some steps, and found the Shinto shrine guarded by two stone foxes. My daughter fed their open mouths the sweet gum seeds she had carried in her tiny hands.

I would later learn the foxes are guardians of the shrine itself — messengers of the *inari*, deities of agriculture, of rice, and of fertility. The shrine, empty except for the air that passes through it, felt sacred to me that morning. Especially on that strangely quiet day. This space in the city created a place for nature to pass through you. The shrine sat nestled in the trees, its placard fallen over from a recent storm. The moss on the north side of the trees smelled wet, like dirt. I thought about all of the dead, all of those we lost so quickly to the virus, all of the spirits suddenly in another place. Sometimes, when I walked through the city that summer, catching the scent of leaves or passing through a cloud of golden gnats, I would feel the touch of those who died and loved the city, those who left so quickly.

The US military base on Okinawa is called Torii Station, named after the Shinto gates at the front entrance. The island came under US naval command at the very end of July 1945, after the battle of Okinawa, where close to 150,000 Japanese civilians and over 12,000 US military personnel died. *150,000 Japanese civilians.* On August 9, 1945, how was it that after nearly running out of fuel, the plane *Bockscar* which dropped the "Fat Man" atomic bomb on the city

of Nagasaki, landed on Okinawa? The B-29 landed with five minutes
of fuel left in the tank, engines dying, without clearance from the radio
tower. The giant cigar, as my grandfather would call it, slammed into
parked B-24s. After all of this, the whole crew on *Bockscar* thought
they were in fact flying the plane the *Great Artiste*. The city that was
supposed to be bombed — Kokura — roiled with smoke from USAF
bombings the previous day. So many facts get lost in the clouds. And
the plane that opened its bomb doors and released the more than
10,000-pound nuclear bomb? On a city that wasn't part of the initial
plan for that day — while it was on the list of proposed cities? It nearly
crashed afterward not on the emergency landing field at Iwo Jima,
but on Okinawa, an island first colonized by Japan and then by the
United States. Now the island is part of Japan but controlled by the
US military.

   I was there. I was there, my grandfather said. *Interviewed to drop
the bomb. A decoy plane. This is classified — I shouldn't —* He stands
up from the couch and walks into another room in my memory.

   How could the name of a military base controlled by the United
States that has been marked with such violence, a place taken from its
history, a place that landed the plane that murdered so many people,
be given such a sacred name?

   Torii Station.

   When I first stood before a torii gate in Brooklyn, that summer day,
I found myself entranced by the shimmer in the water underneath it.
The rippling red beams reflected there. And the stillness in the water.

   Back in my apartment, I look at a photograph of two torii gates positioned as archways above an access road at the US Army Garrison on Okinawa.

Military vehicles pass underneath and through the beams.

You are not supposed to walk directly through a torii gate.

This is where the deity passes.

Introduction

As I write this, global fears of a nuclear threat are boiling over.

At least they are today.

I've noticed that these threats come to the surface and dissipate from the news cycle quickly, as though they were never there in the first place. As though we're supposed to quickly forget this danger. And we do — sort of.

Since the start of the Ukraine War, Russian President Vladimir Putin has been using his nuclear arsenal as a power move. And today, as I cut a piece of bread in half for my toddler's lunch, I saw on my phone the headline from the *New York Times* that Putin is "suspending the one remaining nuclear arms treaty with the US." The war in Ukraine has been happening for about a year. Last year, at just about this time, when February's grayness stretches on and on though some songbirds return to cities and towns, bombed and not bombed, I remember reading another article about a near nuclear crisis. "Putin Declares a Nuclear Alert, and Biden Seeks De-Escalation" I read and panicked. At that time, the *New York Times* reminded us that this was "a heightened alert status reminiscent of some of the most dangerous moments of the Cold War." As in, we are back there, what we hoped was the past but is not the past, *in one of the most dangerous moments of the Cold War.* And then things seemed to settle, at least to the public, perhaps. Settle well enough that the cold grip of fear didn't spread from your heart to your mind over coffee and lodge there. But maybe it did. Or maybe it didn't but should have.

Either way, again, here we are. Knee deep in a possibility. At any moment, a man might detonate a nuclear weapon on another nation, killing hundreds of thousands and igniting a nightmare. You know what that nightmare would be. I'm afraid to write it.

It does not matter who the man is, in a way, now that these weapons exist. It matters that no one uses them. That the wrong person doesn't have them. Different nations have varying ideas about who the wrong person is.

I think about how in the past year there was a run on potassium iodide (KI), an immediate treatment for nuclear exposure. Bottles flew off shelves while people stockpiled it. That happened briefly, and then people stopped talking about it.

I am not an expert in global politics. Or nuclear history. I'm an essayist. And yes, a poet. My scholarly interests in creative writing, literature, and criticism led to a PhD that I finished with grit and sheer will. But I don't see myself as a historian. I see myself as a writer and a teacher. A partner and a mother. A friend who tries not to be late meeting her friends for coffee. I make lunch for my toddler and try not to let the laundry sit in the basement washing machine so the neighbor across the hall must move it. Who am I to embark on this subject, I often ask myself. And yet I have.

I've come to scrutinize the history of nuclear weapons through a personal journey. Why did my grandfather, a pilot in the Second World War, own an unauthorized photo of the atomic bomb cloud spreading over Nagasaki? Why had he said he was there, part of it? And why, hard as I looked, *at first* did I find only a few clues about his war record at all?

What does it mean to have ties to the desert landscape in New Mexico where my grandfather was stationed at what looks like the timing of the Trinity Test before shipping out to the Pacific Theatre during the final stages of the war? What did he experience where the first atomic test spread radiation over the sun-streaked, impossibly beautiful and craggy landscape you might know from Ansel Adams photos, if you haven't been there? And what are the implications for my grandfather's story on the larger historical narrative about the US's justification of using a heinous weapon not once, but twice, on the citizens of Japan? How can I tell this story without inflicting further trauma on communities affected by these bombings while all the same refusing the dangerous mode of silence?

As you might imagine, writing this introduction makes me nervous for many reasons, one of them being linking this book with a contemporary moment that is ever evolving. I hope that in the years to come, we will look back at Putin's threats and remember them as *not* leading to an atomic explosion. This morning, Putin blamed the West for starting the war. And then pulled away from the New START treaty, the treaty Russia had with the US that, according to the US State Department, "enhances US national security by placing verifiable limits on all Russian deployed intercontinental-range nuclear weapons."

A friend sits across from me in a café right now. We haven't talked about this. No one is today. But the threat is all over the news, all over our screens. For now.

Never did I imagine I'd be writing a memoir in part about this subject — the atomic bomb and its nuclear legacy — a subject I don't even like thinking about. Or an introduction linked with such an unstable *now* at the very end of my rumination about how my life has, to an extent, intertwined with this horror.

I needed to write this introduction here, in a café humming with voices. I'm in a city that survived being the first US epicenter of a global pandemic. My friend is typing on her laptop and sipping black tea.

In my poem "H-Bomb" from *Hawk Parable* — a poem about the US's first thermonuclear detonation in the Marshall Islands, which wiped Elugelab off the face of the Earth — the speaker says, "You are about to add a place that is missing so everyone can find it." This book, *The Bomb Cloud*, is about what it means to search for something that is missing. Missing information. Missing stories. And how secrecy creates a violent understory for the narratives that become understood as historical.

And yet, this memoir is, as memoirs are, about personal experiences. But in this case my journey through time and memory as I try to solve a mystery. And become who I am now. The person writing this introduction, who a few hours ago spread raspberry jam on bread before I cut it in half, glanced at my phone, and swallowed the hard truth that again we are at the edge of a nuclear crisis.

In other words, what I know is riddled with shadows about what I do not know.

I think that it is important to acknowledge that sometimes, the truth of a story lives in these shadows. Sometimes, the truth is clouded.

We knew the world would not be the
same. A few people laughed, a few
people cried. Most people were silent.

J. ROBERT OPPENHEIMER

1. Cloud

When you are driving through fog, you trust that the road ahead of you will take you forward. Even though the white curtains don't part around you. Instead, you enter the dense tissue. Disappear into it. Become part of it. You turn your headlights lower so you don't blast the vapor in front of you with light, hiding the tiny stretch of road that you *can* perceive — gray, going, gone — into the cloud.

I've driven on a highway deep in the mountains when suddenly, I've seen nothing but the inside of my car.

My hands on the wheel. My eyes searching the silvery white skeins of vapor smacking against the windshield.

In those moments, my foot on the gas trusts, even wills, that there is a road ahead of me.

I am in the cloud and of the cloud. And I have made the cloud. Well, a part of my story has made the cloud and remains inside it.

When I first saw the photograph of an atomic bomb cloud in my grandfather's album, the almost furry, dark column of smoke, unbroken from its stem, I almost *didn't* see it. It was hidden in plain sight among grainy photos of B-29s and B-17s, among tents, desert landscapes, tropical landscapes, pilots in uniform lined up, and my grandfather as a young man in a jeep labeled *316 BW* (meaning Bomb Wing, I would later learn, and in New Mexico, I would later realize). And there, in the midst of it all, was this strange photo. An iconic image. A horrifying photograph. Unlike the famously reproduced photograph spreading over Nagasaki that begins to break apart, this one was taken shortly before. Maybe a second before. Maybe less.

Yes, this was *the* cloud over *the* city. *The* bomb cloud.

But why did he have this photo? Before he died, when he told me he was involved in the bombing, I tried to net the truth, my questions like intersecting ropes catching at the structure of the story. What I might gather, at that time, turned up empty (or so I thought).

My investigation would lead to clues that suggested possible answers. But these clues also raised more and more questions. And my investigation also turned into a discovery of place. Of New Mexico. And into a discovery of objects that have become historical. Of archival objects. And at the end of all my questions, I found myself confronting the nature of classified texts themselves and how blanked out stories shape the shadows of history.

I've driven deep into the mountains of New Mexico when suddenly, all around me, ice and fog wrap the trees. The trees I *can* see are now dripped with diamonds of ice. Dangerous. Distracting. The air swirling around me smudged thin and white.

Did he lie? I was sometimes asked after my grandfather's death. I would answer that I didn't think so. Deep down, I knew that he didn't. But now I'm as certain as I can be that he was telling the truth.

This is a story about an erasure — many erasures. The erasure of peoples, places, and facts that cloud the development of the atomic bomb. I make no claim to fill in the gaps. What I have done is to articulate the shape of the cloud that obscures them. To notice the holes at the fence so that when I peer through them, I understand my limits and also what else might be outside of my frame of knowledge.

And so, this story, this memoir, holds the truth as I could best find and understand it. And in this story is a violence of mind-numbing proportions. A violence that has touched us all.

Much farther into my investigation, as I stood outside my car in the caravan outside the Trinity Atomic Test Site, engine running, waiting to show my ID, I noticed the low clouds skirting the mountains. White, hazy in the morning desert light.

But as the clouds lifted, I realized I could still see them — and the shimmer belonged to white sand.

2. Boom

A STORY OF ERASURE, ACCIDENT, AND EXPOSURE IN THE
NEW MEXICO DESERT

Mountains curtained the sky ahead of us. Spring hadn't arrived,
but the sun blasted the paling road, the finch-feather grass, and the
torches of evergreen all the same. Time seemed suspended — but not
in seasonless sunshine. Instead, I passed through something like time
on the Safety Corridor on 502 to Los Alamos. As I rounded a cliff,
light splashed over my shoulders, and like hose water, all over the
hood of the car. Oppenheimer vacationed here in what he thought of
as "impossibly remote" terrain. Before the shock wave. Before the light
became something more than light, visible only the instant the blast
cooled just enough for the cameras.

Cameras captured the images we know: the bulbs, the mushrooms,
the turrets of clouds. When you are here, in New Mexico, where the
potential for infinite destruction all began, you feel like you are in
a photograph. But seconds still tick at the wrist like blood sluicing
through a vein.

Before a tower dropped the Trinity bomb in what is now the
White Sands Missile Range, boys put frogs in each other's beds at the
Los Alamos Ranch School in cabins that would later become ad hoc
labs and workshops for plutonium. This was before the facility
became a campus, before the town gridded into housing developments
and grocery stores.

Before we burned our way into a new geological epoch.

Before everything changed.

On your way into town, the landscape leading into Los Alamos opens up to cliffs that frame the sky like a shag haircut. An ice cream scoop could have carved the rock out, and all the trees clinging to it in the wind hardly move — gnarled, twisted. Here, beauty is a word that arrives in the mind slowly, the way water boils an egg. Except for the make and model of the cars swerving past you on the corkscrew turns, and maybe except for the oddly warm winter — hardly any snow since January, which will mean more summer wildfires — the charged quality of the air tricks you into thinking you're back in time seventy years. If there is one spark, one cigarette, one blue pinprick of static at your sleeve, one open can of gasoline, could all of this vaporize?

The name "Los Alamos" means *the poplars,* more specifically the cottonwoods that pour into the sky. The nuclear facility hums here, though you can't hear it. Everything around it pushes you away gently. You can enter the small science museum for free. You will not be tempted to purchase a book because the bookstore went out of business before you arrived.

One rare afternoon, the Los Alamos National Laboratory's presence announced itself in Santa Fe. That winter morning, I was sipping mint tea in front of my laptop screen hoping to settle the question mark curling in my stomach. All of a sudden, I heard a roar. Everything became part of the sound, its color a deep blue. My mind smeared like light between the stardust whorls of the Milky Way.

Did a massive engine blast past my building then vanish?

I thought about guns. Military jets.

I went to the window and touched the glass. Cold. Sun grazed the roofs of the cars in the lot below me, and beyond them, the field where prairie dogs burrow into the earth stretched out emptily. No one in a puffy vest and neon hat wandered down into the arroyo. The mountains rose like a stage backdrop, this time peach under a pale blue sky. Nothing. January was January, and I returned to my desk. The shape within me had grown a silky pelt of hair. I shivered and wrapped my cape-like synthetic sweater tighter around myself. Nothing stirred.

The size of a pea pod, my secret could open and close its mouth and fists.

Out my window overlooking the road, a U-Haul swerved around the bend, broadcasting the graphic of another state on the side of the truck. Colorado, a bighorn sheep. And so, the New Mexico mountain town became ordinary again.

But what really happened, I later learned, was anything but ordinary. And a bubble seemed to form around what exactly it was.

The Santa Fe Fire and Police Departments, as well as New Mexico Gas, fielded phone call after phone call from worried residents.

"Everything shook, like a pressure wave went by," writer Brian Dear tweeted.

✛ ✛ ✛

At the Buckman Road Recycling and Transfer Station, Ross Muir told a reporter that the walls around him shuddered. "I thought it was a jet ... I kept waiting for a parachutist to come floating down."

Whatever ripped through town felt so out of place that we had a hard time describing it.

That moment when a *thing* roared past our city and into the Santa Fe National Forest, all of us became linked by wonder, awe, and fear.

The Los Alamos National Laboratory did, eventually, claim the sound. What we heard was an explosion — one that was "routine." *Routine?* I thought. The lab is not allowed to test atomic bombs. After the Comprehensive Nuclear Test-Ban Treaty of 1996, the United States does not detonate nuclear explosives underwater, in the atmosphere, or underground. What could this explosion have been, and why? The Lab holds radioactive materials onsite. The vessels tempt summer wildfires that edge worryingly close to town and wash the Pojoaque Valley in a yellow-tinged haze.

"Boom" read the title of the email that went out to companies and news organizations in Santa Fe a month later, on Valentine's Day. This time, we were warned. The Santa Fe Police Department issued the notification:

> *Advisory: Expect a big "boom" between 1 and 3 PM this afternoon.*
> *Los Alamos Labs is doing some explosives testing. .*

Testing, dot, dot — with an ellipsis point missing.

The final mark of the pause? Unfinished. Like a thought trailing off and breaking even as it drifts away. Like a rip in a plume of smoke.

The Los Alamos Ranch School, founded in 1917, became the location for "Site Y," the secret lab for designing bombs. After the war, Los Alamos could be entered only through a checkpoint. Now, you can drive into town, park outside the Bradbury Science Museum, and take photos with your phone.

I planned to wander Main Street. I imagined chocolate shops and treelined walks at Central Park Square. The dune-colored map outside the Bradbury Science Museum suggests a green space. But the Central Park of Los Alamos instead squares into a parking lot surrounded by a strip mall of white flesh buildings and teal roofs. Sun beat down, like mallets on metal, onto the walls. Percussively bright. But there was hardly a sound. The park was vacant.

It is true: I did not visit the town during a farmer's market or 5K race or Halloween parade, when people would be more likely to fill the park. But the emptiness that afternoon — *everyone must be somewhere else,* I found myself thinking — felt so real I wanted to shout something just to hear my own voice bouncing back and forth between glass storefronts and offices. My shadow lay down on the brittle grass and pooled over the sidewalk as though I could leave it there.

The Los Alamos Ranch School thrived until 1943. Before that, crops clung to the craggy, sun-beaten landscape. Between 1887 and 1942, a number of homesteaders — Miguel Sánchez, Benigno Quintana, Harold Brook and his mother Mattie Brook (who homesteaded acreage bought by Harold), and A. J. Connell — set up small farms on the Pajarito Plateau. Harold Brook applied for land in 1908 and over time bought eight hundred acres. So dedicated to tilling the dry soil,

Brook became known as "Bean King." Just about ten years later, after financial setbacks, he joined his assets with a man named Ashley Pond. But Pond wasn't interested in farming after all. He wanted to start a boy's school for the children of wealthy New England families. So, Pond bought out Brook, whose lungs eventually swelled with blood.

I learned all of this on the Los Alamos Homestead Tour, which is self-guided and involves reading placards placed in various locations in the park. After you cross a parking lot, you can step into the spare shadows of deciduous trees that know better than to unfurl their leaves just this side of the last frost. Structures appear — a couple of log cabins. Come closer, and you can read historic markers with labels like "Site 1," "Site 2," "Site 3." How similar these names are to weapons test areas.

Homesteaders and other private landowners had to sell their lands to the government as part of the war effort, reads one placard.

Had to.

And then, *in their place came the men and women who designed and built the world's first atomic bomb.* I think about what *in their place* intends to excuse.

What would a placard look like that stated what actually happened?

✣ ✣ ✣

I first visited Los Alamos when I was *expecting,* a word that indicates the hope of something to come all the while acknowledging that it might not be so. I stretched to hold the energetic little body that bounced off the walls of me and pressed footprints into my ribs.

Even after losing two pregnancies, I carried this presence — my third time trying to thicken with tissue — I imagined looked like peony petals to a town constructed over the hidden enclosures of radioactive waste. The Los Alamos National Laboratory was already so close to Santa Fe, where I lived and went to prenatal appointments, that the 17,500,000 square feet of radioactive waste the Los Alamos Study Group says is "disposed" on-site could poison me and the secret growing inside of me. The Las Conchas Fire of 2011 edged close enough to the lab that it could have very well compromised the safety of everyone living in the Land of Enchantment.

Just over three hundred football fields of nuclear waste decay in Los Alamos. I read on the Los Alamos Study Group website that the lab "continues to generate and dispose of radioactive waste on-site at a facility called "Area G," which is the largest MDA (sixty-three acres)" — MDA meaning Material Disposal Area — "and contains the most waste (10,800,000 ft; enough to fill 1.4 million 55 gallon drums)." This waste sits within a twenty-minute drive of the Santa Fe Plaza. I don't want to think about this. I read that the Los Alamos National Lab has plans to "expand MDA-G by sixty-six acres, more than doubling its size;" I learn that "Indian ruins lie in the expansion path," the study choosing this way to refer to Indigenous Peoples. In a section of a report by US Department of Energy Office of Environmental Management titled "Synopsis of hydrologic data collected by waste management for characterization of unsaturated transport at Area G," some of the "borehole" sample included "Tsankawi layers." Tsankawi is an Ancestral Pueblo village. The Bandelier National Monument west of the laboratory, where you can hike Tsankawi Trail, holds stone stairs and sacred petroglyphs.

I think of the narrative crafted about the Los Alamos Homesteaders on the self-guided tour: "in their place [or, *after the US government requested that they leave and claimed their homes and land, displacing Hispanic and Indigenous communities,* I want to scrawl in sharpie in the margin] came the men and women who designed and built the world's first atomic bomb."

When an atomic bomb cloud shoots skyward after a single neutron triggers a chain reaction inside a metal shell, what vaporizes? What appears when dirt and dust and steel fling away from the blast epicenter — only to be fenced off, given a narrative, controlled?

The secrecy folded into the Los Alamos National Laboratory forbids our imagination from perceiving what it means to live and work so close to masses of toxic substances that approach our idea of infinity. And from what it even means for this place to exist and who is left out of the story.

Since the general public doesn't have access to the full knowledge of this site, what specifically happens with waste materials, and when they become consigned to the earth, we skim a word like "disposed" (the nuclear material "disposed" on-site) and buy into its definition. *Discarded. Thrown away. Cast off.* But the material is still there, on location like an unconscious memory.

I want to think that because we've created islands of swirling plastics in the Pacific Ocean, humanity is just beginning to learn how there is no *away.* Believing that we've learned from our mistakes when there isn't evidence of this and that we will overcome the disaster we created for ourselves is yet another way to push a mess of facts into deeper waters.

✛ ✛ ✛

I imagine a landscape untouched by toxins. And I searched for one in the sun, in the cottonwoods, and in the blue streaks that clouds draw over the mountains. I looked for this place in the shadows while I drove on roads with names like Oppenheimer Drive and Manhattan Loop.

Against disaster, the town of Los Alamos leverages parks, schools with good rankings, and mountain-view roads winding to large homes and townhouses.

Trinity Drive is the name of the main thoroughfare. A world-destroying bomb named after the Father, Son, and Holy Spirit. And now, the Godhead Road brings you to McDonald's, Smith's supermarket, Holiday Inn Express, and, at the edge of town, to the Atomic City Transit hub, where you can "dial-a-ride" if you miss the bus and find yourself waiting too long under the dry, cold starlit sky.

The Atomic City, by name, promises the irreducible. Something at the core of what we are. Atomic City Quilts sits innocuously across from the Bradbury Science Museum. Electron symbols orbit the atom, planet-like, in the logo fastened to the khaki-colored storefront that offers bolts of heart-shaped cloth for quilters. Atomic City Radioactive Hot Sauce blends the region's red and green chiles in a warehouse north of the Los Alamos National Laboratory. And the Los Alamos Project Main Gate, a white shack with the famous sign that insists "PASSES MUST BE PRESENTED TO THE GUARDS," is not an entrance at all — other than to some clean toilets within the gutted tourist landmark. After you wash your hands and step outside the renovated shack, behind you is a chain-link fence and what looks like a parking lot.

Behind it some unmarked buildings, and then a stratified outcrop. Beyond that, mountains.

Layers upon layers.

Unlike Roswell, New Mexico, which glows neon with alien kitsch, Los Alamos spreads out into bland, identity-less buildings. The nuclear laboratory nowhere and everywhere.

"Now I am become Death, the Destroyer of Worlds," Oppenheimer famously said after witnessing the Trinity bomb explode. Along with the potential for ultimate destruction, Oppenheimer did destroy worlds — individual worlds. Children and grandchildren taken from their land. Residents — largely Hispanic and Native American — who lived near the Trinity test claimed by cancer. Mothers living in the downwind zone losing their infants.

Oppenheimer also said, "My two great loves are physics and desert country ... it's a pity they can't be combined." In Richard Rhodes's *The Making of the Atomic Bomb,* the author spins Oppenheimer's statement: "Now they would be."

The Trinity bomb explosion would shower radioactive particles across the state. Physics and the dry ecosystem of the Pajarito Plateau would become indelibly fused. But love — the desire to care for, protect, and cherish? While Oppenheimer did not know exactly what the Trinity bomb would wipe from the Earth, he did know that one love would envelop, transform, and forever change the other.

That I may rise and stand, o'erthrow me, and bend
Your force to break, blow, burn, and make me new.

A place can be empty, beautiful, and dangerous.

Saw my first roadrunner today. It strutted in front of my car on I-25.

I found this note in a journal when I was looking for scraps of information I compulsively scribbled down when I visited the Bradbury Science Museum in Los Alamos — the museum filled with photos of Oppenheimer, plus a statue of him that you can approach and look in the eye.

But my note about the roadrunner — the bird that moved like a shadow in front of me — came from a moment of my commute through the Santa Fe National Forest to the former railroad town of Las Vegas, New Mexico, where I was teaching. At least one student died each spring, when wind barreled crosswise over the interstate and wild temperature swings tempted seedlings to sprout early. Hail and slush would pummel everything.

In my notebook, underneath my bird observation, I dashed a horizontal line across the page in black ink. Then, *My student's friend died on the road on Sunday. The wind killed her. She lost control of her car, and it rolled multiple times in the median. She was a softball player. My student went out looking for her and found her when she didn't come home to the dorms. Taught elegies tonight.*

The car upside down. Jason Aldean still singing from the stereo. Grieving friends. Grieving parents. The community pall.

Every spring.

Boulder-sized brush tumbled across the road. The shrubs

wouldn't bend, hard from generations of these seasons. As you squint into the sun, a crosswind shoving the car, you might let go of the steering wheel with one hand to brush hair from your eyes, to reach for a water bottle, to glance at your phone.

Where are you? the message might read.

Uranium is in the drinking water in Las Vegas, New Mexico. City reports indicate that this uranium comes from "natural deposits." Nonetheless, I think about the three hundred football fields of decaying nuclear waste an hour and a half from the water fountain across the hall from my morning classroom. In New Mexico, the proximity to Los Alamos, the region's history of uranium mining, the legacy of the Manhattan Project, and the continuing weapons tests render the dangers of radioactive substances almost illegible. The state's economy depends on both the Los Alamos National Lab and the Sandia National Laboratories. As investigative journalist Claire Provost writes in the *Guardian,* while the town of Los Alamos "has more millionaires per capita than almost anywhere else in the country," it is "surrounded by some of the poorest counties in New Mexico, one of the poorest states in America."

A former colleague in New Mexico would bring coffee in a vintage mug of milky green uranium glass — called "Vaseline glass" — to meetings. We would sit around a seminar table together. The mug came up to his mouth, then his lips touched the uranium, then the mug would come down, and his thumb would fiddle with the handle.

When I commented once on being in a room with with this mug, everyone laughed. Yes, I read that that these antiques "are usually not a health risk if they are in good condition." Glassware can be dangerous when chipped — dangerous for the person drinking from it.

But The Environmental Protection Agency's report on "Radioactivity in Antiques" indicates that for at least twenty-five generations (or two thousand years), that mug would be "hot."

When my pregnancy began to show, I'd rub the moving being inside me, the life that would become my daughter, while observing this colleague lift his cup.

Driving around Los Alamos, I got out of my car and stood at the curb of one home in a new housing development, aspens glimmering around me. The little knife-like leaves would bronze in autumn. Families live in these expensive, large-windowed houses, the land all around them swallowing human-made radioactive substances. Parents work at the lab. Children attend Mountain Elementary. One of my students had grown up here.

Her father worked as a nuclear security technician of some kind. Without him, she told me, the safety of everyone in New Mexico would be compromised. I believed her.

Recently, in a fluorescent-lit room honeycombed inside of the Los Alamos National Laboratory, an accident that killed two scientists shortly after the end of the Second World War almost repeated itself all over again.

Nine months, a human gestational period, after the United States eviscerated Hiroshima and Nagasaki — even after scientists witnessed an atomic cloud shudder over the New Mexico desert and wondered if they had ended the world — Louis Slotin, a young scientist in Los Alamos, wanted to show off how to test plutonium's threshold of criticality (when there is enough plutonium to activate a chain reaction). "Tickling the dragon's tail" is what scientists called the trick. Instead, Slotin dropped the screwdriver he used to keep the beryllium shell, which looked like a hollowed out half of a globe, slightly apart from the plutonium pit protruding from the other half of the split sphere. When his screwdriver slipped, an eerie blue light, called a "Cherenkov flash," glowed in the room. He shielded his audience from the light as best he could and died from radiation poisoning at age thirty-five, just over a week after the experiment.

Nearly seventy years later, for a recent photo op, technicians arranged eight rods of plutonium on a table in a building named PF-4 in the Los Alamos National Laboratory. In PF-4, too many rods too close together waited for the camera flash. As near to one another as they could be without reaching criticality, the rods would have shone with an odd blue light if one more bar had been placed on the table slightly differently for a striking visual composition.

Someone in the room recognized what was about to happen and quickly moved the rods apart.

No one evacuated, which is what should have happened.

I read about this close call in *Science:* "[Doug] Bowen, who was then Los Alamos's top criticality safety expert and now supervises safety work throughout the weapons program, recalls getting a phone call about the technicians' error from an assistant lab director around ninety minutes after it had been discovered." An hour and a half. You can watch Jean-Luc Godard's *Breathless* from start to finish in the time it took for the person in charge of nuclear crises to learn that a deadly situation had almost happened.

The beauty of New Mexico is one of high contrast. Sun and shadow, water and dirt, sky and mountain. Explosions and silence.

"I was born up on 'the hill.' But I don't even remember living up there. It's a weird town. Best described as a company town, the way it was then. They had a library and a police department, but not much else," John Barton told me. Barton is an architect in Santa Fe whose father visited the high desert outcrop as a boy with Barton's grandfather. While casting fly-fishing lines into eddies of glittering water, his father fell in love with the way the sky blued above him over the baked earth. And so, later as a young man with a family, his father jumped at the opportunity to work on the nuclear bombs the United States would develop in Los Alamos and test throughout the '60s in Nevada. Oppenheimer, Fermi, Slotin, and Niels Bohr — all colleagues. And then he moved his family out of town, to La Puebla, shortly after Barton was born.

"I went to high school in Los Alamos for one year to see what it was like. There was one kid in my biology class who was making a bomb to blow up a pumping station and lost his hand. He blew himself up in his garage. His dad was probably making bombs, like my dad was making bombs."

Los Alamos boasts skiing, hiking, and scenic overlooks. Yet the scenic town also contains "34.7 square miles of Department of Energy

Property," the lab publicizes. Fenced off, monitored, not open to the public. One of the Los Alamos National Laboratory's main objectives — still the same as the early years after the Second World War — is to guarantee that the United States' nuclear arsenal is ready to explode at a moment's notice.

New Mexico's beauty and what it cradles among its windswept mesas — families, communities, ecosystems — are now positioned at the precipice of a self-destruction so total that all we can do is acknowledge the façade that distracts us from our ruin. Here is an Atomic City alive, not *the* Atomic City in Idaho, nearly vacant half a century after a nuclear reactor exploded and killed three men whose bodies became so toxic loved ones buried them in lead, steel, and concrete. Here, the town seems clean, quiet, industrious. Before you visit Los Alamos, you might think you will get close to the "campus." You might wonder if you will see a building that guards vats of energy. Inside these vats, the possibility of hundreds and hundreds of momentary suns. Secret City Kitchen offers sandwiches off Diamond Drive. Your coffee brewed with tap water originated in the city aquifer, nestled with a plume of cancerous hexavalent chromium. The lab tests the feathers of poison.

Assures us that all is well.

✛ ✛ ✛

It happened one ordinary winter morning after the New Year, on a day I chipped away at my to-do lists after the holidays. Ice on the windows. And the flutter of tiny feet stirring inside of me. This was the third time I grew a heart with my blood. Then a sudden swell of sound enveloped me that, for a moment, blotted out all life. I was gone. Everything was gone.

Then it all came back again.

This test, this explosion from the nuclear lab, wasn't supposed to reach our ears, our muscles, our bones. What blasted from the lab had become an accident.

On the phone with me, Barton was adamant. "But the lab gave up doing any kind of explosive tests years and years ago," he insisted. "They used to test explosives in the canyons to the south of town."

Used to, we all like to think.

"A Los Alamos National Laboratory statement said it was unusual for its blasts to be heard off-site, but this one was heard all over Santa Fe — about twenty-five miles away as the crow flies — and as far east as Eldorado and as far south as La Cienega," stated the *Albuquerque Journal* after the event.

The secret split the air open and left us empty.

The day I strolled through Los Alamos, queasy from the hands and feet pushing out of my skin, I stepped past the placard about the history of the town and approached a log cabin. Could I open the door? No.

This was the Romero cabin, built by Victor Romero for his wife, Refugio Sanchez. One room. Six children. The Romero family lived off the land, growing beans and corn.

But then Technical Area 55 swallowed the cabin's original location.

I'm not allowed to kick up the soil where gardens once held seeds or pace the original perimeter of the home before the walls, like Dorothy's in the *Wizard of Oz*, lifted up and landed here. And neither are Romero's descendants. I later discovered on a map of the technical areas of the Los Alamos National Laboratory that Area 55 is now a "Plutonium Facility Site."

So, a team preserved the cabin and moved it to the center of town. Here it is.

Empty. Now the Romero family's house sits in a park next to a strip mall. Where cattle grazed, where Refugio wrapped tamales, and where her children played with balls of alpaca yarn lives a different house with its own generational legacy. There sleeps a substance that looks like tarnished silver.

This substance infuses what it touches with its presence and lives forever.

The first atomic bomb ever detonated exploded near a country's own civilians. Soil melted, famously, into radioactive glass. The US government combed the Trinitite out of the crater. And tourists? Banned from collecting the green nubby shards.

Nonetheless, the Earth expels this gemmy substance. Insects "push beads of Trinitite up into the sunlight, a memento mori in ravishing green glass," writes Richard Rhodes in *Smithsonian Magazine*, who adds, "The shards left behind, embedded in the Earth, surface as though to remind us that the story is not finished, not whole." What we have created, unintentionally, is a dialogue between nature and time, legible even when we stop digging into the core of who we are. And what we've done.

The "War Department" wrote a letter to the Los Alamos Ranch School. You can read the words a typewriter punched into paper in December 1942 on display at the Bradbury Science Museum:

It has been requested that you refrain from making the reasons
for the closing of the school known to the public at large.

✛ ✛ ✛

So, a military complex appeared suddenly in the mountains, with no explanation. It hardly mattered that history had been erased and rewritten. We accepted the story. And now, a lab occupies this place in New Mexico as though it had always been here. But everywhere and nowhere, in the earth and in the sky, there is poison you cannot see, touch, or taste.

An atomic bomb is like a star. But it takes away all life.

After I heard the explosion that ripped through town, I imagined the needle of a jet flying high over Santa Fe into the jay-blue sky. Now, I think of the sound as a shape. The sideways 8, infinity, that a jet could script into the sky with smoke and oil.

If the end is often the very point where a story urges you back to the beginning, what do we do with a substance that is both beginning and ending?

The swell of a sonic boom looks like the fan a boat drags behind it through the water. My shape, as I grew, shuddered with this sound. I held this life inside of me, and the boom held me inside of it.

When I commuted to Las Vegas, New Mexico, I found myself accidentally going eighty-five miles an hour, as fast as a truck slamming into a wall in a FEMA test for radioactive waste packaging. On occasion, I'd drive ninety miles an hour and pump the brakes when I'd see patrol cars around the bend in the piñon. Sometimes, I flew even as the shape inside me grew, forgetting I was carrying more than myself before tapping the brakes and tugging the vehicle back down to seventy-five miles an hour.

At the edge of our solar system, our sun's plasma creates a bubble for us filled with wind and stardust. When my cell signal cut out, I could have left the world.

3. Afterimage (I)

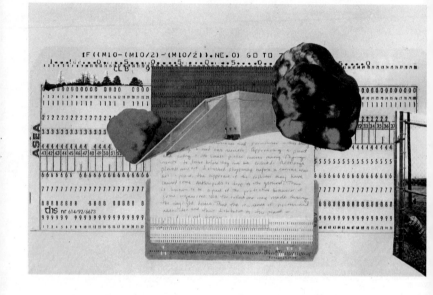

Object description: Mixed-media collage. Trinity blast cloud reproductions. Insect collection records for the Nevada Test Site (1962). Fence from the Los Alamos Labs with the back of a worker digging in the dirt. Tree line near one of the pits of earth dug for the labs that would contain "sensitive" material (radioactive). Computer punch cards cut up, excerpted. Background: computer punch card enlarged. Camera bunker built to protect the equipment that would capture the very first atomic explosion the world has known. The camera bunker? A triangular shape.

4. Backdrop

When I heard the wind, I knew my daughter would not sleep. From
the motel window, Taos Mountain hid behind lavender snowfall
swinging thick fluff around its muscles like a towel. My daughter
bit my areolas with her two bottom teeth. She squealed, happy, when
I winced.

That day, I counted her wet diapers, stained sunflower yellow,
and worried she lost nourishment among the prickly pear and cholla
as I walked with her strapped to my chest. High desert afternoons fall
thirty degrees at sundown and bring snow rolling off the mountains.
My daughter had stopped drinking from a bottle or cup. For weeks
now, she only wanted me — my skin on her lips. The sugar from my
blood in her mouth.

The New Mexico wind can sound like a choir. It hummed into the
cracks in deep windows, mud walls, and carved doors. Instead of muses,
the night brought dissonance. I thought of the other being I carried
and lost right before my daughter's cells clung to me. I had proudly
displayed the photo-booth-like images of that child-that-wasn't-to-be
for visiting family who would cautiously say, *Ah, how sweet.* From
a town nestled in the Cerrillos Hills, I'd bought a tiny terracotta bud
vase that rocked in my palm like a toy. *For my table,* I'd thought. The
mouth would be perfect for the petunias I would later let starve on
the deck, the pink and yellow petals fluttering in the wind before they
began to wither like light leaving water.

My daughter, at nine months old, breathed the air of the desert
as long as her lungs swelled with my fluid. Like so many others who

came before me, I watched the mountain furrow with clouds, the fissures looking like trails the mind can touch.

In a photo of my great-grandfather, young, in Bohemia, he proudly poses for the turn-of-the-century studio portrait. New bicycle (stage prop), bowler hat (stage prop), he stands in front of a parlor that is actually a painting of a parlor. The corner of his mouth turns up. *All this is my life now,* his smile seems to say about the pose itself. Then he left Kožlany and his family of weavers.

A photo I texted my mother a month into my daughter's life shows the infant plucking the yarn of a blanket like a harp. My mother crocheted this for her. Ribs rippled through the baby's upper back. I did not make enough milk. The pediatrician, rather than urging me to supplement with formula, instructed me to increase my supply. *Take fenugreek pills, pump after you nurse, eat avocado, suck down the "Pink Drink" at Starbucks, check the latch, check the latch again, do not let the baby nap while she nurses, eat oatmeal, bring her into your bed, do not bring her into your bed, meditate, massage your breasts, invite someone to stick needles into your chest, find women who can give you their extra breast milk.* I followed advice from the pediatrician, lactation nurses, and Internet message boards.

At the doctor's recommendation, I met weekly with a lactation nurse. The perky woman pointed with claret and glitter fingernails at a breast-shaped pillow, sang *nipple to nose,* grabbed my baby's head, and shoved her face into my chest. *Try football hold!* she commanded.

I broke like a field pocked with prairie dog holes. I broke like the cottonwoods cracking limbs off in the wind that scatters them around the roots. Like prayers from mouths in a cemetery.

I broke like a skull.

My brain confused my daughter with one of the wouldn't-be-children. Smiling in her stroller at the park, she would look at me with her marble-blue eyes, and I would say, *That summer I lost you, I ...* She shifted the shadows of the fir trees off her newly plump legs.

On Halloween, three and a half months after a doctor sucked her out of my birth canal with a vacuum, my daughter finally reached three percent on the growth chart. I had supplemented with Similac.

This afternoon, when I opened a café door, I smelled raspberry incense and weed. The wide-eyed barista mumbled, *We're closed today,* while she observed a man strum loud chords on a scuffed ukulele. Instead of writing, I returned to the motel, lifted my tank top up, and exposed myself. With her new bottom teeth, she took me in her mouth, jerked her chin back. Moons bloomed around my nipples. Not all nights arrive with stars.

5. Home

"Go home," I said, as though to myself.

The dog, black as a tire, stood in the middle of the street and blinked. Wild dogs in town belong to no one and hunt for bar trash in packs at night.

I knew this dog. It wasn't wild. It slept in a wire pen outside the house on the corner.

The autumn sun flared so bright it danced in psychedelic squiggles. People like to say the air in New Mexico is "the cleanest you'll breathe." Seventy years ago, the Trinity test exploded subatomic particles all over the dirt and into the livestock, the wells, and the throat like a vampire kiss.

Up, up, and away.

Two months ago, I moved to a town where the sidewalks chip like teeth. The concrete blocks in Las Vegas, New Mexico squeeze up against one another as though an earthquake had jostled them a little out of place. Green-white weeds decorate the cracks where the crickets hide to sing *death, death* — that old song. The Sangre de Cristo Mountains — *blood of Christ* — lie like flesh all around the highway out of town. Their redness settles down when the sky pinks the evening and you drive through it at eighty miles an hour.

I would often pass the dog as I sprang from a walk to a run, rounding the corner, looking down now and again at the disturbed sidewalk. Day or night, the animal would be lying on the baked ground, a shadow of itself, eyes open, curious but noncommittal. Some kids had bent the blank street sign at the corner, the words bleached out by sun. The green square points straight up like the launch mechanism of a heat-seeking missile.

Here, like a lot of small towns, autumn brings football, the faint cheers pulling excitement into the breeze. Mesquite smoke stinks in a gray and delicious way through the air. Autumn brings high-school lovers holding hands in the alley between our house and our landlord's house. Yucca shadows stretch out so long on the ground that if you snapped a photo of them with your phone and showed it to someone back home, they'd think it was almost winter. The sun can make everything look cold even when you sweat through the sweatshirt you've thrown over your head.

Autumn brings a kind of lust, the leaves curling on the ground like death's confetti, the best part of the party almost over.

The town sits 6,424 feet above sea level, high enough to follow the special baking instructions on the box. My afternoon runs here are small victories. Even climbing a flight of stairs can make my lungs feel like two plastic bags. Lightheaded, my brain detaches from my skull and hovers three feet above my head while I catch my breath.

"Go home," I said again.

The dog was still squatting in the middle of Fifth, not taking a shit, just sitting there. A rusted-out Chevy rolled through the stop sign as though its engine pistons were in a stupor. The driver stared openly at me, his white hat moving with his entire head. Up and down. Tits and ass. He rolled down his window but drove on, around the dog. It stayed.

Women don't walk alone here — unless they're bringing a child into a gas station or the post office. I didn't have one, but some of my students did. "Get a bike?" our landlord's wife offered when I told her I planned on walking to work.

The dog's eyes were wide-set, its nose flat. I thought it might be part pit bull and part black Lab, the expression puppy-like even though it had to be over a year old. Beautiful animal.

We thought about renting the yellow-and-white stucco house where the black dog now sleeps in its pen. We looked to rent it in July. Mice had chewed binocular-sized holes in the wall next to the kitchen sink.

"They won't give up lightly," we'd laughed. So, we moved into a house down the street. The yellow-and-white house sat vacant for a few weeks, and we never saw anyone do work inside. Then two people — a retirement-aged couple, I heard from our landlord—moved in anyway, in September. The dog was theirs. Sometimes a man in his twenties sat on the front steps smoking in the dark. We'd say hi to him when we walked past. Maybe the dog was his. Maybe it wasn't.

Batman — obviously not my spouse's name — had admired the glassed-in front porch. He still seemed wistful when we walked by it. He liked to imagine himself sitting there with a telescope pointing at the blood moon, or Mars near dawn. I liked to imagine us together inside the glass room looking out.

✢ ✢ ✢

"Well, that was a first," I'd called into our living room a few days earlier, shutting the front door tight behind me.

The cats, used to me leaving the door open so they could sniff through the screen of the storm door, looked a little confused. They meowed a couple times, then disappeared.

"What?" Batman asked. He was tinkering with an electronic device on the floor, keeping himself busy building a guitar pedal. He thought he could make more and sell them to a music store in Chicago.

"I was hollered at right outside our house."

My spouse stopped what he was doing and looked up at me. I still can't read his gray-blue eyes sometimes. This frustrates and enchants me.

"I'm sorry, hun," he said. He looked worried now.

This wasn't the city life we knew. All of it — the gun shops open on Sundays, the mirages pooling the highway in quick patches that disappeared, the nosebleeds — new to him. He used to whip around the racetrack loop of the DC Beltway, thumbs only on the wheel. He used to race up the Kennedy Expressway to O'Hare, in and out of step vans and trucks, in record time to pick me up. (Did you know the Kennedy has an average Yelp rating of two stars?)

Out here, among the sage, and the spiders dropping from the ceiling in invisible threads, and the nights so quiet a couple of barking dogs become an orchestra of sound — but this story isn't about that.

Sundays, I leave Batman home and run out my anxiety. The house — a living space larger than we'd ever rented — had become his fort. A whole empty corner of the living room waited for use.

I've noticed that on Sundays, ranchers come to town. They eat at the diner that presses pig fat into its tortillas. The diner employs the girls from the high school whose fathers let them work weekends. Before their shift, in the fluorescent-lit bathroom at the back, they mask their faces in orange foundation that ends, like childhood, in fingermark streaks at the jaw.

Sundays, the men come to eat nursery bundles of flesh drowned in green chili, and then cruise around town, looking for girls while church bells ring.

Sundays, I find myself running.

When you drive Interstate 25 out of the town of Las Vegas, New Mexico, you find scrub pines clinging to the cliffs with a timelessness that feels prehistoric. The windshield frames the landscape like a Polaroid. Red rocks that have tumbled to the road from the outcrop appear just as the sign warns in its pictogram of little black shapes.

It is impossible to tell what season it is unless snow crusts the pines and transforms the terrain into the craters and mesas of the moon. Without snow, during any other season, the light dusts everything in an ahistorical visual imaginary.

Tourists love doing this drive. It feels like you're a protagonist in a movie, like *Easy Rider* or *No Country for Old Men*.

Maybe because this place hasn't been touched by time (except that it has), camping is a way of life. Pop-up trailers hitched to trucks carry hay-smelling mattresses through the Glorieta Pass between the mountains.

When my dad was a kid, my grandparents took the family across the country in a VW bus. They showed my siblings and me the carousel slides from their trip on a sheet pinned to the living room wall. As the slides clicked from image to image, I'd fold and unfold my socks, exposing my heels as though I were thinking about wading into the sea.

The brown-haired boy in a funny hat, the boy that looked like my brother, was and was not my father. He was and was not standing in front of blue-white ice in Glacier National Park. The glacier was and was not there. Was and was not becoming not-there.

When twilight comes to the blank edge of town, where Walmart appears before the hills, even the cerulean-joined shopping carts turn their wheels into assemblages of regret. Finally empty.

✛ ✛ ✛

I feel so far away, I typed in an e-mail. Did I delete this or send it?

✛ ✛ ✛

The dog stood in the middle of the street, looking at me. *Fine,* I thought. *Stay there.* And I did the little kick that starts my run — past the yellow-and-white house, past its chain-link fence where the black dog usually sleeps, past a rock garden the weeds reclaimed, past the house with the camper out front with "For Sale" scrawled in Sharpie on a piece of cardboard taped to it, to the corner where the street turns into a one-way and the land belonging to the high school begins.

Grasshoppers sprang at my ankles, their metallic wings parting like scissors as they bounced off my skin and socks. Hitting the concrete, the bugs sounded mechanical, like tiny robots that have cameras inside of them and tracking devices and will explode on impact.

When I reached the high school, I felt like I was being watched. But the street stretched ahead of me: No one was out. During the week, the high-school marching band walks around the block. The booming drums and horns seem to come from everywhere and nowhere. Batman knows their routine like clockwork. Last Friday, I happened to be home from work at three p.m.

"What *is* that?" I called into the house, swinging my bag off my shoulder and onto the floor.

"That," said Batman proudly, "is 'Uptown Funk.'"

"No way."

"Yes! Listen." He scooped up the new kitten and cradled him against his chest, waiting. Then with his free hand he pointed, cuing a choir. Then, "Don't believe me just watch!" he sang in falsetto.

Sundays, the kids were doing what they do — getting high by the river, maybe. But I still felt it, a presence.

I looked behind me, and there he was — the dog. He — I don't know why I decided he was a he — had trotted behind me for blocks, dipping in and out of my shadow. He was my shadow.

"Home!" I commanded in a mean voice. "Home!"

My little shadow cocked his head, his eyes bright. I noticed he had slightly square ears.

"Home," I said more gently, the *mmm* lifting from my lips like ash.

"Home," I cooed, the way the dentist says, "Almost done," while his sharp tools needle your gums.

I pointed back down the street. The dog looked at the tip of my finger, like dogs do, with the curiosity of an astronomer waiting for a planet to appear in the sky.

The sun was setting earlier these days. But the empty afternoons still caught the light where no one sat outside on lawn chairs, or played the Top 40 on the radio from the garage, or walked up Sixth with a paper cup of hot coffee, or sat on the church steps where there was a tombstone "for the unborn."

Later, I would flop over the twisted sheets of our bed, my sports bra sticking to the *Split This Rock* T-shirt with the collar cut off. I would grab my iPhone from the vaginal dip in our white blanket. I remembered a conversation I had recently with another writer. Cell phones can't be in poems, she'd argued. I admired her commitment to this idea.

Random q, I would text, closing my eyes and waiting. *Ding.*

What? My friend responded. I was lucky to catch her on a weekend afternoon.

If you could be any superhero, who would you be? I typed, not sure why I added a comma to the introductory clause.

Idk all the female superheroes are blah. I think I'd be xena warrior princess, my friend responded.

Haha yes. I can def see that, I wrote.

Then she asked, *Who would you be?*

I hadn't thought about that. The Red 40 blackout drapes bloodied the afternoon light on the wall like a wet maxi pad.

Hmmm though I don't particularly like Catwoman I think I'd be her, I finally answered.

:) if only Catwoman weren't objectified I'd totally be her.

I'd pull some shorts and a T-shirt from the bottom drawer of the rickety baby dresser I inherited and have been using my entire adult life. A moon-faced, bald cartoon of a man leers at you from inside the drawer. My sister or I had drawn him in pencil.

Later, I would pass a man from town that looked friendly. I would leave my city smarts somewhere. I would make eye contact, and smile, trying to feel a part of something.

"I'd have a piece of that," he would say. He'd say it as though to another man who wasn't there. There is always another man almost there. He made disgusting, lip-smacking *Mmmm mmm* sounds with his mouth. *I'd have. That.*

Have. He said it like he was folding the corner of a page of a paperback for later. It made my lungs fill up with blood. *That.* I did nothing. I passed the empty university football stadium, its arched gate chained and padlocked.

✤ ✤ ✤

Four days before Thanksgiving, the dry leaves and warmth on my face would make me think again of early October, always terrible in its beauty. Batman married me then, a frat boy assaulted me then, and every year I look forward to passing through the season as though I'm moving through a tunnel. Here, in their sameness, the days sat on my chest like the incubus in Fuseli's painting. I couldn't "shake it off," though Taylor Swift told me to in my headphones.

My shadow dog was not with me then. I felt both alone but also not tied to the ground.

At a waitressing job in my early twenties in small-town Pennsylvania, the bartender would say "I'd love to see you in a leopard-print thong" for the audience of bros watching baseball on TV. The cook would slide behind me and flick my hair. At least he burned Béla Fleck songs for me onto a CD. At a department store job, where I worked as a "floater" (like a speck in the eye), straightening shirts and dusting pewter frames waiting to be engraved, a man asked me a question at the perfume counter one night, so I'd leave the glass moat of expensive bottles. He let his wife walk ahead of him. Then he grabbed my hip, pulled me closer to him so I could smell his grassy breath. He pinched me and winked as I opened my mouth for the nothing that came out.

I was running under some maples at the back of campus that looked like they'd never turn yellow, no matter how many days you could X out of the calendar. I passed a house with the Greek Jesus fish painted on its stucco side. *I'd have that.* The man's words were still ringing in my ears.

I moved my gangly body — with my gasping lungs and funny hair — down the road. I labored around the corner, over the absurdly high curbs while bugs stuck to my socks. I kept running, to the little plaza in the center of town, to the gazebo where people with guitars sing sometimes to the newspapered windows of empty storefronts all around them.

A red car paused in front of me, and a guy — with his teenage voice — yelled from the passenger window, "Yeah, baby." Something stupid.

"Fuck you!" I yelled. Then I gave the whole car the finger.

They didn't expect that — I saw one kid's face, and he looked insulted. They drove off, but in a few minutes, the car looped back around through the traffic circle.

Okay, I thought. *Here it comes.* But no one said a word as they passed me, slowly, staring.

One of the town squad cars that polices the plaza, to make sure people really are driving fifteen miles per hour, rolled by. I half expected him to give me a public profanity citation. For all I knew, I'd yelled at one of the county judge's grandsons. But he left me alone.

So I ran through the empty street around the plaza and back, crossing a bridge over a creek that is almost always dry, where two hot rods were parked. A large man in his twenties was drinking a red concoction out of a Pepsi bottle. Two girls in cutoff shorts that, as my seventh-grade science teacher used to say to us, were like a report "long enough to cover the material, but short enough to keep things interesting," giggled into their cupped hands.

I weighed my options. I could run into the street with my back to oncoming traffic and the slighted car of teens on the loose, or I could run through the narrow but passable chasm between the man and the girls and say, "Excuse me." I've done that before.

"Excuse me," I said, and ran through the thin gap between them.

"High five!" the guy said, holding up a meaty hand.

"Sorry!" I said, having practiced this universally magical performative speech act with success before. The apology can f orce the other person into acceptance of you, your state of being. *No money. Sorry. So sorry.*

Silence. I passed through it.

Then, "No problem! CUNT!" The word trailed after me. CUNT.

His pervy lips put it in the air, and it stayed.

Cunt. It fanged me in the back, between my shoulder blades. It always makes me feel lucky, being called a cunt. I think that is what I hate most about it. Lucky it isn't something worse. *Cunt.* It could be worse. Might be. Instead of wings that push you forward as you run, it embeds a hook in your spine that links with a fishing net that pulls in everything about that moment and, instead of making it yours, makes it punishable. Theft. *Your fault,* I could almost hear someone saying. This is our space. Ours. *Your fault.*

One night in Chicago, after the Blackhawks barely won a tournament game, I was walking in the dark back to my apartment with Xena. We heard voices calling after us.

"Megan, Megan, it's me!" A man in his twenties, sloppy drunk. We both looked around for Megan. He had a friend with him.

"Megan, it's [Mike / Matt / John] from the bar! I gave you my number. Megan!" He was headed straight for me, his hands open. He was pleading. His friend grabbed him.

"It's not her. It's not."

"Yes, it is. MEGAN!" He tried to fight off his friend.

I guess I can look interchangeable. Long brown hair (without as much silver then). That night, I was wearing a white shirt and jeans. *Basic bitch,* I've heard. Xena had short blond hair with a blue streak in it. It had been raining, and I was holding an umbrella with the Velcro flap undone so the metal bones draped the fabric like a bat sleeping upside down, wings almost open.

"I'm not her!" I yelled back. Did I also yell, "And I'm married!" and hate myself after?

Maybe.

"Megan!" he called. "MEGAN!" As we walked away, we heard, "You stupid bitch! You stupid bitch! You stupid bitch!" He screamed it. Screamed and screamed. Xena and I broke into a run.

"Stupid bitch!" followed us.

✛ ✛ ✛

Even typing out "cunt" makes me mad. I was texting Xena. One of the cats made a *prrrt* sound and jumped on the bed. She likes the smell of sweat and came to lick my arm.

I waited. Then, *ding.*

Xena: *I hate them with the fire of a thousand suns. I hope they all get testicular cancer and have to have their balls amputated.*

Xena's rant became a curse. *I hope their houses are in foreclosure or they get evicted from their apartments. If they have kids I hope their kids become drug addicts and never accept help and break their hearts and they are forced to bury their children.*

The sun stained the walls of the room red.

I felt rage and sadness.

✛ ✛ ✛

On a drive down to Alamogordo, I arrived at a town on the map that marked the emptiness with gas stations and auto repair shops half burned down, some with blown-out windows.

✛ ✛ ✛

There are so many stars visible here the sky looks like spilled sugar.

The darkness can make your hands disappear in front of your face.

After a night class, I would open the car door and look up. Where are they?

There. The Seven Sisters. Pleiades: I would look for it like I was looking for a friend. I liked seeing it up there, almost hip-like, a small geometry of mischief above my car.

The pinhole lights flicker like a cell phone in a movie theater. They move faster than you think. If you look away for a minute, thirty seconds, you'll feel disoriented when you look back up. So much flickering.

It all tilts, as though without you.

When I was opening my car door one night, home from class, I saw a stray pacing in front of the house. It wasn't a dog I recognized. Not my shadow dog. Not Brooklyn or Chewie, the dogs that belonged (if that is the right word) to the Rastafarian community across the street. Chewie liked to sit on top of the white Camaro rusting out its days inside the fence. Sometimes Batman caught Chewie and led him back across the street. Our neighbor would appear from behind the tapestry hanging where the door would be. "Love to you," he'd say, tapping his chest with his fist before taking the rope.

This dog was different. Wandering. Wild.

Even though it was so dark I didn't know where to put my feet, I could see this dog's little white teeth, its eyes.

I froze, my key in my hand, the jagged ridge between my pointer and middle finger. What women do with their keys. What we've been taught to do.

Breathe, I told myself, my key stupidly ready.

The animal paused and backed up. I could hear its nails click across the road — away, almost gone. Batman opened the front door then, flooding the gate with light.

He always waited for me at night.

✛ ✛ ✛

When the weather finally started to turn, I noticed something. The town seemed quieter. The dogs that barked at the darkness, that slept in front of the houses on our block, had disappeared.

I hadn't seen Chewie edging backward on top of the hood of the Camaro. I hadn't seen my shadow dog either — not for a week at least. I had seen animal control's white van slowly cruising our street.

"Did you hear about the ordinance?" Batman asked, coming home from Walgreens with red wine. He'd been gone a long time.

"What's going on?" I was sitting at the table by the kitchen window with my notebook and had seen him chatting with our landlord before coming in.

"No one can chain their dog up out front anymore. There's a big fine. And animal control is rounding up dogs and issuing citations."

"That's good," I said absently, writing a phrase on the page that I'd cross out later.

"Home?" I'd asked, skipping across the street. The dog wagged its tail, mouth open. Happy pink tongue.

It had only guarded me that one time. Is guarded the right word? Wasn't it inflecting my movements with freedom? Annunciating my flight?

I haven't seen the dog since. Not in its pen, the mud still dented like a pillow pressed in from a face. Not in the road. Not as I ran.

Or had I? Seen it?

I was merging onto the highway out of town to make the hour trip to Santa Fe to stock up on groceries. The sun ringed the windshield. And I began seeing them.

Shapes of fur. Little mounds, like sand. Dogs that had been flung out onto the highway from windows. Encouraged to slip from the back of pickups. Or pushed. Left dead in the margins like advice. Red. White. Black. Fur in the sun. Splayed. Split guts.

I saw mouths open in a whine, tongues touching the road as though to say one last thing.

Love.

I saw a white dog with legs bent so far back they had to be broken, the wind ruffling its fur. It looked like the stray that hung around where the hoarder lived, its eyes red as two smashed raspberries. I hadn't seen that dog in a while.

And then I saw a black dog with square ears, its eyes closed.

It looked like my dog, my shadow. I couldn't be sure.

The animal's round face was shoved at a weird angle. Its ears perfectly still squares. I blew past it, a shadow in my rearview mirror. Smaller and smaller.

✣ ✣ ✣

"Home!" I sang, and he followed me, farther and farther away, the day stretching before and behind us like cirrus clouds.

We ran as *home* became any other word, just as empty or full.

"Home!" I lied, the word becoming a game. I lied and lied. *Home. Home.*

The dog followed me, and we pranced down the road together toward campus, meeting a few other strays — the white dog with red eyes that stood outside the house with metal chairs stacked all over the yard. Past the chihuahua that never barked but used to approach my ankles as we ran.

Past the ranch house with the iron fence painted Pepto Bismol pink at the tips, as though that's where Puff the Magic Dragon got gored.

Skip, skip, his nails clicking on the concrete. A pickup with a cord of wood in the back and a man in a cowboy hat at the wheel stopped and waited for us. No one whistled at me, at us. We kept going, past the abstinence education center across from the daycare, past the school natatorium with the algae-green water and a "No Stalking Permitted" sign taped to the glass doors. When I stopped, the dog stopped. A few times, when I looked behind me, I couldn't find his shiny black body. Once he stopped to sniff for mice around the tires of the orange Dodge Charger blocking the sidewalk.

When I returned the dog — finally, after all our fun — to its house, I noticed the "No Trespassing" sign fixed to the side windows. Those signs must have been there when we looked at it that summer. I knocked on the door of the glass porch and heard rustling inside, but no one answered. I walked as far as I dared up the driveway, leading my shadow with me, until I released it.

When I walked away, I felt like I'd dropped something on the ground behind my heels. I looked back and saw nothing. Not a part of myself. Not the dream.

My feet could lift up with each step into the high-altitude atmosphere.

My lungs would fill, finally full.

"Home," I said, as though to myself. The word left my mouth like breath.

II.

1945

After months of work, both day and night, we were ready.
The Air Force built a tower and installed still, movie, and high-
    speed cameras.
The impulse was timed to arrive at zero-minus-one minutes.
[Cropped hands adjust control knobs]
We were prepared with color and black-and-white instruments.
We set up a delay for each one.
We took 12 still pictures per second.
We captured 96 frames per second.
We captured 12,000 frames per second.
After, our units shut off the cameras to avoid destruction.
In this type of work, a half-second would be considered a relatively
    long delay.
During practice tests, all problems were overcome.
This made possible the image of the actual event.
An action too fast for the human eye.
[A volcano erupting underwater]
We made the slow-motion picture.
[Watch]
The world with comprehension.

6. Afterimage (II)

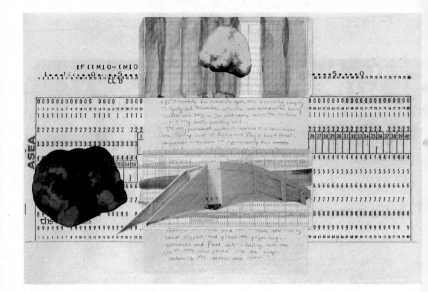

Pretty colors, like a child's bed sheets. Popcorn ball shapes. Before my father took us to the movies, my mother would melt butter into popcorn and stir candy into it. My father would smuggle these bombs of salt and sugar into the theatre for us. In the dark, we bit into them like apples. Pink. Yellow. Light from the screen.

The top punch card was one of the first I painted while I worked on the series. I stained each of the columns except for the "% enrich" and "isotope" categories. This card would have recorded radioactive material. The card below it, ribboned pink and yellow, would have recorded employee work hours. The camera bunker tilts on top of it. (Triangular shape.) The magenta bloom looks like the bunker flicked it away. Is it heavy? Does it float?

7. Periphery

I knew that when I passed the easy-to-miss sign for Carrizozo, New Mexico, I'd be approaching the latitudinal zone where the Trinity bomb was detonated on July 16, 1945. Just under a month later, a US pilot dropped an atomic bomb on Hiroshima. Days later, another pilot dropped an atomic bomb on Nagasaki, which my grandfather said he saw in the air.

"I was there," he insisted. My grandfather told me a group of men from the government interviewed him to be the pilot to drop "the bomb." After his death, I discovered a photograph of the atomic cloud spreading out over Nagasaki in his album from the war.

When he gave this album to my mother, he told her, "This was classified."

But there is no evidence to back up his story. I lose hours and hours staring into the screen of my laptop and wade into the vapor of his claims, until I find myself staring into buggy websites once maintained by aging veterans. A graveyard of memorabilia sinks deeper and deeper into the network of the Internet search engine. I've ordered flight rosters I can get my hands on from interlibrary loan. I do not find his name. He said he was part of the mission, yet I've combed through what USAF records are limitedly available in the National Archives online database and keep finding nothing. Because of his aunt's address book, I know he trained as a pilot in Alamogordo, New Mexico before shipping out to the Pacific Theatre.

Alamogordo is a military town at the edge of the White Sands Missile Range and the powdery dunes of the White Sands National

Monument. I drove along the eastern perimeter of the weapons test site as I headed south. I wanted to understand what it might have been like for my grandfather to be stationed so close to the gypsum dunes, so close to where the first atomic bomb would be detonated. I imagined I might learn about his connection to the Manhattan Project and his role in atomic history when I was there. .

In his other photos in the album, you can see the shadow of the planes on the ground above thatched roofs. There are blank squares in the album where a few of my cousins pried out pictures of my grandfather posing in the cockpit. This was the night of his funeral. But no one touched the picture of the mushroom cloud.

My grandfather liked taking photographs in motion from the plane. In one, the runway looks like grooves in snow as the plane touches ground. The wings are behind you, behind the lens.

Why did my great-aunt cross out the addresses of her seventeen-year-old nephew instead of erasing them? She left his whereabouts legible — footprints I try to follow.

For miles and miles, there is nowhere to turn off 54, which is the bare road that hugs the perimeter of the White Sands Missile Range, an active weapons test site. Ground zero for the Trinity Test atomic explosion cannot be seen from your car. When you cross the latitudinal zone, cell service cuts in and out. There? Pink and brown land, crusted with ice. Farther south, the ice melts.

In a press release, the Army claimed that the Trinity bomb drop was an "accidental" explosion at a storage center for ammunition and weapons. In music, an accidental note creates a change that can be so sudden and strange it alters everything for a moment, or for a sustained period of time. Through the swell that takes over the original key, an entirely new system seems to emerge. Then the wave of it all settles back. Sometimes.

"Gadget," the nickname for the first plutonium device ever detonated, became a code name in the lab. When it went off in the Tularosa Basin of the Chihuahuan Desert, physicist Kenneth Bainbridge turned to J. Robert Oppenheimer and said, "Now we are all sons of bitches."

When I traveled to Alamogordo on the barren stretch of winter highway, I felt like I was transgressing a hidden boundary. The atomic pit nests inside the White Sands Missile Range like a heart in an anatomical drawing. In my memory, the site stretches out in a silvery slab. On Google Maps, it looks like a gray box.

My memory is surely affected by the black-and-white photo I took with a disposable camera when my car crossed the area approximately perpendicular with the test site. It is not a "good" photo. I extended my arm out as far as I could. My other hand firmly on the wheel, I locked my eyes on the gray streak ahead of me. No cars ahead. I was concerned about ice on the road. I wanted the camera to record what it saw independently of me.

Here is the blur of landscape. Here is the relative self, moving — moment to moment — through the world. Then, *out of the corner of my eye*, as the expression goes, I glanced at the land. The edge of my eye saw what the lens saw. This. Or not quite this:

I pointed the lens at what I couldn't see, aiming aimlessly. I could not see the plutonium bomb crater, or the pond-green glass melted into mottled rock. I let chance do its work. My finger pressed the button.

Chills raised the hairs of my arms. But after a while, my body stopped reacting, and I drove on, numb. On Google Maps, Earth View, you can see the obelisk marking the very first nuclear test, which *ushered in* — a phrase that makes me think of funereal suits — the nuclear age. When you zoom in, the monument looks like the monoliths that gave the primates in *2001: A Space Odyssey* the knowledge to murder one another.

It was like being at the bottom of an ocean of light.
We were bathed in it from all directions.
— Joan Hill, physicist, on observing the Trinity explosion.

✛ ✛ ✛

Days before my journey, I looked at my route while the TV glowed.
My laptop warmed my legs. I zoomed in and out of Google Maps and
dropped the little yellow guy — *why are we supposed to imagine a
man entering unknown territory?* — down into areas of the weapons
test site not grayed out. Perhaps this NSA-authorized view of the
site is meant as a kind of compensation for the secrecy that for so
long cloaked the atomic explosion thirty-five miles from Tularosa,
New Mexico.

The mayor of Tularosa has said, "I don't think there's a family in
this community that hasn't had a loved one die of cancer."

The US Department of Energy Nevada Operations Office
published a bulletin in 1994 that was revised in 2000 called *United
States Nuclear Tests: July 1945 through September 1992*. The cover
of this document shows two photographs: an explosion of sand that
looks like live coral blooming upward, and then the resultant crater,
half in shadow. Reading the bulletin, we learn that the crater is called
"Sedan Crater." We see, on the copyright page, that "Sedan Crater was
formed when a 104 kiloton explosive buried under 635 feet of desert
alluvium was fired at the Nevada Test Site on July 6, 1962, displacing
12 million tons of earth. The crater is 320 feet deep and 1,280 feet in
diameter." Where did the "12 million tons of earth" shooting into the

sky of the first photograph go? The red soil and robin egg sky make the radioactive earth something beautiful.

The report organizes the names of the nuclear tests in a variety of ways. You can read them according to date, according to location, according to purpose. And you can read them alphabetically by their names. The "T" names begin on page 142. I am relieved not to find my name there, after "Tweed," detonated in the Nevada Test Site on May 21, 1965, and "Tybo," also detonated in the Nevada Test site but ten years later, on May 14, 1975. Trinity, one of three tests conducted in New Mexico, appears in this section. The other two tests in New Mexico exploded near Carlsbad and Farmington.

According to the US Department of Energy's report, *United States Nuclear Tests: July 1945 through September 1992*, "Unless otherwise noted, all nuclear tests at the Nevada Test Site or the Nellis Air Force Range (NAFR) to September 15, 1961, produced radioactivity detected offsite."

I appreciate the following "Caveat" paragraph of the report:

"The information contained in the document has been gleaned from multiple sources over time. Some of the data has been updated to reflect the most recent analysis conducted by the national weapons laboratories. When discrepancies were encountered, every attempt was made to use the most acceptable or verifiable information."

When discrepancies were encountered, every attempt was made to use the most acceptable or verifiable information.

This disclaimer could be an epigraph of an essay. Or a memoir.

✛ ✛ ✛

Why did I go in January when I could have visited ground zero in early autumn, when the leaves scatter in the street? Or I could have stood in the spring air, warmer to the south, the pink light filtering into my hair. Visitors attend the biannual "open house" on the White Sands Missile Range in early April or early October on the two days a year it is open to the public. The reason I didn't go then during my first journey there was that I wanted to experience the boundary of the missile range as I drove and see what anyone might see on any other day. Instead of being walked into the White Sands Missile Range as a guest and looking at the lava monument to the blast where "Gadget" dropped from its hundred-foot tower, I wanted to explore the eastern perimeter of the missile range. I wanted to think about boundaries and who decides when they are permeable. When are you allowed to cross inside, as a guest? What becomes of you, inside that boundary? I would go through two checkpoints and enter the White Sands Missile Range, still an active weapons test site, on a weekday. I would go to the warhead museum.

I braked on the highway, the car skidding on the ice. When I stopped, it was like time stopped, the stillness sharpening all around me. I yanked the wheel left and turned myself around, thankful I didn't waste too much of the gas I rationed. There was a town between here and there: Vaughn, New Mexico, population 438. Because I was traveling alone, in winter, I wouldn't stop there.

Cows had recently frozen to death in the scraggled fields near where I started my journey. I had been living in a former railroad town on the Southwest Chief Amtrak line, Las Vegas, New Mexico. Trains still come and go there, their wails drifting over the boarded-up buildings and scrap yard if the wind is right.

I heard about the winter deaths on the radio while I zipped my snack bag for the drive. *Bring water. Bring sandwiches. Bring blankets.* The squall came fast. Ranchers didn't have time to bring the animals in.

The January sun emits a certain kind of light in the desert that promises darkness — the sky purple at four p.m., with any lingering warmth pulled away with it. The brilliant glitter touches you, cold. You are the *nothing that is not there and the nothing that is* of Wallace Stevens's poem "The Snow Man."

Before my trip, I imagined myself parking my car on the highway and crossing into the weapons site on foot "to see how far I can get." But as I drove, the invisible line punctured now and again by "no trespassing" signs became as real as a glass wall.

Some friends in Chicago wanted me to download a "Find My Friends" app so they could tap the icon on their phones designed to look like a piece of leather sewn onto the heel of a hiking boot and see me — the glass-head pin of me — edging south.

"The app won't track me," I tried to explain. My cell phone would break connection with the nearest cell tower.

If they checked in while they rode the Blue Line out of the Loop, or hopped off the Western Avenue bus, I would disappear. Then I would reappear. Then disappear.

✛ ✛ ✛

Have you ever seen a feathery shadow at the edge of your eye?

Was it a figure? Did it cross into your vision, like a hummingbird there and gone?

When you press the button of a disposable camera, the mechanism letting in the light clicks quietly.

Almost as though nothing happened.

I chose a disposable camera for the photographs I would take along the edge of the missile test site because I wanted to excuse myself from artistry — and because I wanted to engage with the idea of waste.

I wanted the stark light of a New Mexico winter to interact with the film. I wanted the mechanism inside the plastic case to open the lens like an eye blinking. I wanted the world to appear on the film, helped by me as I traced the edge of a mass of land marked off for the practice of destruction.

The camera would come with me though the checkpoints I would cross to enter the White Sands Missile Range.

My grandfather is not on any of the official rosters of the Nagasaki squadron of planes: not *Bockscar*, not *The Great Artiste*, not *Big Stink*, not *Enola Gay*, not *Laggin' Dragon*, and not *Full House*.

In the album that my grandfather gave my mother, the photograph of the Nagasaki detonation — "Fat Man" — shows an aerial view. This photograph does not duplicate the famous aerial image of the cloud cap detached from the stem. But it isn't an amateur image either. I can't be certain how he acquired it, but I don't think this cloud came from his camera.

His photo shows the bomb blast a fraction of a second, or a full second — a breath, a heartbeat — earlier. The blackened column hasn't split. It opens into a puffy top. The image looks solid. As a form, it evokes unity.

A photograph cannot even come close to representing what it is like to see an atomic explosion in person.

Scientists who witnessed the nuclear tests of 1946 in the Bikini Atoll couldn't adequately describe the Operation Crossroads detonations.

"One reason why observers had so much trouble in
retaining a clear impression of the explosion phenomena
was the lack of appropriate words and concepts.
The explosion phenomena abounded in absolutely
unprecedented inventions in solid geometry," wrote
William A. Shurcliff in an official report.

Photography isn't allowed on the White Sands Missile Range. I
wanted to steal a couple of shots of the warheads. I remember going
to the gypsum dunes — white in peaked mounds like granulated sugar
that look like slopes of beach sand — of the White Sands National
Monument before I stood in the field of bombs. But the episodes
happened in reverse.

From White Sands, you can see San Andreas Peak, 8,235 feet,
and Gardner Peak, 7,533 feet. The brochure I picked up at the
national park's visitor center promises that the landscape will
"shimmer." It does. When the sun strikes the sand, it looks like a
mound of finely crushed diamonds. (I have never seen a mound of
finely crushed diamonds.)

The White Sands National Monument became a consecrated space in 1933. In 1942, the land around it became a "large military land presence," according to the timeline provided by the National Parks Service. In 1945, the first atomic bomb ever exploded detonated in this "large military land presence" all around the park.

The sand feels cool, even cold, when you bend down and press your palm to the seemingly bleached surface.

The moment I stepped out of my car in the national park adjacent to the missile range, I needed to touch the impossibly white grains because I felt like I stood before a screen. I stepped into the screen, becoming part of the foreground. Sand verbena and skunk-bush sumac scratched into the static I felt extending all around me.

"Do not tunnel into the dunes; they can collapse and suffocate you," warns the brochure you pick up before you drive into the white silence that almost tingles in your ears.

The imprint of the sea is still here. Your nose detects water. As you spin around slowly, you see more and more of the dunes that roll on like sun-white waves. The dunes become imitations of themselves, molding into more and more forms. The eye searches past these iterations for sheets of water.

The boundary around an active weapons test area — a governmentally authorized dangerous place — presents a narrative. Outside of it (even just outside of it), you are safe. No one can hurt you — or at least the thing *inside* the boundary can't. The boundary might be a fence with barbed wire. It might be marked with signs but otherwise seem like an empty, sloping landscape along a highway. You might not see anyone or anything for miles as you drive along it. You might not even see the fence itself as it edges further inward, as though the hand drawing the box of it in a plan bumped — as though the person drew it into existence on a piece of paper while riding inside a combat vehicle.

"Borders are set up to define the places that are safe and unsafe, to distinguish us from them. A border is a dividing line, a narrow strip along a steep edge," writes Gloria Anzaldúa in *Borderlands / La Frontera*.

A recent report in the *Wall Street Journal* of all places reproduced a diagram to show "Radiation levels after 1945 Trinity Explosion." The graphic looks like a topographic map with concentric bands of color. Yet the shapes do not represent altitude. The colors represent roentgens, the unit of measure for gamma or X-rays. A roentgen measures the energy in a cubic centimeter of air. Ground zero of the Trinity explosion in New Mexico after the blast on July 16, 1945, looks like a red, oblong shape. Exposure? Ten roentgens per hour. An orange oval around it? Two roentgens per hour. I notice that Alamogordo is not on this map, even though it is the closest city to the detonation center. The graphic also lacks a black tick to represent the Holloman Air Base or the area where pilots and their families live. Las Cruces, the next nearest city southwest of the testing area, is also not on this chart. But Las Cruces was not downwind of the explosion like the town where I was living, Las Vegas, New Mexico. The ranching and former railroad town sits in the top tip of the .1 roentgen exposure area. Albuquerque and Santa Fe? They are in the .01 exposure area for downwind radiation on July 16, 1945.

Ranchers whose families have lived and worked in Otero County, New Mexico, for generations continue to live outside the edge of the missile test site where the first atomic bomb exploded. Their animals graze on the "safe" side.

"For years, residents of the rural, heavily Hispanic villages near the test site have claimed that a mysterious wave of cancer has swept through this dusty stretch of south-central New Mexico, decimating families," states Dan Frosch's article "Decades After Nuclear Test, US Studies Cancer Fallout" in the September 15, 2014, *Wall Street Journal*.

People drank radioactive milk from the cattle that grazed in the fallout zone.

Alfalfa growing in the field edging the White Sands Missile Range becomes food for the ponies standing in shiny clusters nearby. The young animals look like ellipses dotted with a calligraphy pen onto a paper bag.

✣ ✣ ✣

"Communities are to be distinguished, not by their falsity /
genuineness, but by the style in which they are imagined,"
writes Benedict Anderson in *Imagined Communities*.

+ + +

One section of land in New Mexico, the White Sands National Monument, is a "great natural wonder" says the National Park Service website. Adjacent to every edge of it is another area of land, the White Sands Missile Range, which is so huge that it touches five counties in the state and serves as a government-sanctioned space for test rockets and non-nuclear explosives. The border between pristine space and trash space is not visible to the eye — other than a sign here or there as you cross it. On a map, it looks like one box sits inside another box.

The communities that live around the White Sands Missile Range and downwind from the "Gadget" epicenter did not count as being worthy of the truth the day fallout showered the earth. The "accidental" explosion had been planned for a place near the poor, the nonwhite. It is as though these communities simply hadn't been imagined at all in relation to the "safe" / "unsafe" boundary by those in power. That is the same as being imagined disposable.

+ + +

At 2:00 on a Tuesday afternoon in January, I travelled White Sands Boulevard out of Alamogordo. Motel 8s and Holiday Inn Expresses lined the road. The motels are for pilots' hook ups, but also for family members when the base opens for visitors. White Sands Boulevard becomes US-70 and takes you to the checkpoint for the Holloman Air Base, where I saw an F-16 darting through the fabric of the sky.

I hadn't prepared myself for the language of the sign I saw when I exited US-70 and entered the access road for the White Sands Missile Range at the southern edge of the entire test site.

"ENTERING ACTIVE TEST RANGE," you are warned.

"AREAS POTENTIALLY CONTAMINATED WITH EXPLOSIVE DEVICES."

"STAY ON ROADS."

My plan, which I had written down in a notebook as though that made it official somehow, was this: *You will drive with the White Sands Missile Range to your right. Somewhere between hour two and three, you will cross the longitudinal point where the Trinity Test detonated. You will get as close as you can.*

But this plan emptied out and became a gray, monotonous shape once I crossed the region and continued driving to Alamogordo and then onto the access road to the weapons test site.

You will get as close as you can would mean navigating a boundary. I would experience the perimeter as an edge I would see out of the corner of my eye, and I crossed it at the point where such a crossing is possible.

"During World War II, the US military tested weapons in the dune field beyond the park," reads the *Exploring White Sands* brochure. The test site and the park's histories are intertwined. The "Operating Hours & Seasons" page of the White Sands National Monument website designates a section for missile tests still conducted there:

"Due to missile testing on the adjacent White Sands Missile Range, it is occasionally necessary — for visitor safety — to close the road into the monument for periods of up to three hours. US Highway 70 / 82 between Alamogordo and Las Cruces is also closed during times of missile testing."

I imagine my grandfather bombing the dunes.

The sand had long blown over his footsteps.

✛ ✛ ✛

Visitors are not supposed to touch any debris. It can still detonate.

✧ ✧ ✧

"Bring a coat out to the dunes," the college student working in the visitor center warned me. "The temperature drops twenty degrees out there."

As I walked down the first path, the Primrose Picnic Area, I laughed to myself. I was wearing all black, absorbing the brilliant sun. Even the insects that live in the gypsum sand become powdery white. I must have looked like a shadow in my black pants, black boots, black coat — my pale hands and face disappearing.

At each trailhead, visitors are supposed to sign a book housed in a wood hutch. A string attaches the pencil to the pedestal, so it doesn't blow off. Rangers check for missing hikers at sunset.

I didn't sign my name in the log because I thought I'd wander out and only climb one dune. I also liked the fantasy of losing myself. Of never having been there.

As you turn around, you might forget where you started. You might walk away in the wrong direction.

I find myself doing this, again and again with this project. I turn around, and as I do, I encounter what I can only describe as the sense of the infinite. What ends, and where?

Why don't I have enough evidence, a map, a clear narrative? Each dune looks exquisitely the same. Each clue leads me into a landscape that is always shifting around me.

A story. A photograph. Dead ends.

I walk out into the snowy sand.

✧ ✧ ✧

The off-ramp led me to the main gate that loomed ahead like the stage of a music festival: the arch reminded me of scaffolding for theatrical lights. I saw a visitor lot on the right next to the small office building where I knew I'd need to check in. *Watch for rattlesnakes,* warned a sign.

The United States does not detonate nuclear weapons as tests anymore. But all kinds of chemicals shoot out from rockets and missiles. Another sign warned me against touching anything. I didn't see any debris.

The ZIP code for the White Sands Museum & Missile Park is 88002. Infinity, infinity. Zero, zero, And then two: me and you.

As I stood alone in my body on this weapons test site with the enormous mountains in the distance and the reddish brown dirt thrown around them for miles in every direction, I felt fear, regret, and panic. I didn't want to be here, yet it was my plan to come. I couldn't hold onto the illusion of safety that the area just outside the boundary offered.

I entered the office building of the visitor center. The door opened to a room that reminded me of the DMV: beige floor, beige corded phone on a particleboard desk. Sun filtering through a dusty window curtained the air like smoke.

"Good afternoon, ma'am."

A man in an "I love Jesus" hat with "love" as a stitched heart greeted me. He had been sitting to the right of the door.

"Hi," I said, looking around the room. I had brought the various kinds of identification required to access the site, and I had even finally gotten my new driver's license in the state of New Mexico for this purpose. I hated the new picture, so I kept my old license in my wallet as well. I handed everything over after I sat down. My feet tapped the floor involuntarily.

We made small talk while the man inspected my materials and typed something into the old, beige PC. I remember saying I was here to look at the gypsum dunes. That wasn't true. I remember saying I was a writer and laughing it off. We talked about how the sunset would look on the dunes.

"Smile!" He took my photograph and printed out a slip of paper I would present at the checkpoint to enter and leave the missile site.

Then his eyes scanned my face — my eyes, my nose, my lips, which I pressed together and quickly cleaned with my tongue — like he was scanning a barcode.

"I'm running your numbers now."

"OK," I said.

"I get people talking," he said. "They forget what I'm doing because I like to ask questions and get them to say things to me. If the FBI wants you, you won't even know I'm calling the police until they get here."

"Oh," I said. I tried not to sound unintentionally sarcastic. I had no idea how I was supposed to respond or what affect was expected from me.

"If you have a warrant out on you, you should stop me now."

I felt my expression going blank. Then I smiled. "I'm wanted in all fifty states!" I joked.

He chuckled and said, "Well, good. We have you now."

Was he profiling me during our entire conversation? Probably.

Then he flashed me a smile that showed two gold teeth I hadn't noticed before. I felt guilty of something, but I had no idea what.

"There. Now you're in the system," he continued to say as he typed. I let him — type. Put me in the system.

I am in the system, am part of the system — the system that made all of this.

In the photo he took of me, I look half sheepish and half relieved.

I felt empty, with a kind of existential horror.

My mother told me a story her father once told her about the dunes. When he was stationed there, he took "a girl" out into the white sands in a jeep after sunset, which was against the rules. Numerous lipsticked women appear with him in photos. He wasn't very tall, but his seventeen-year-old face looks rugged and strong-chinned. His eyes either seem sad or filled with mischief in his photos.

So, he snuck one of the vehicles out. Who was the young woman? I don't know.

The gypsum dunes stretch out into the desert for 275 miles.

The ring of mountains around you mimic one another, shape after shape, among the white mounds. The forms of the Tularosa basin seem to copy themselves, and then copy themselves again. The gentle sloping dunes pour out around in piles like salt.

Before the sun set completely, when it rubbed the edges of the mountains with pink pastel chalk, my grandfather drove out into the dunes with a young woman and probably a bottle of liquor in his pocket. He drove with one hand on the wheel.

I don't know at what point he realized he lost himself. That kind of realization comes slowly, as the landscape becomes more and more like a white lie.

Drive around this dune, and this one, and the ring of mountains marks your spot. And then this one, and the stars rise. Did he tell the woman?

All I know is they spent most of the night driving. At one point, he thought he'd never find his way back. But they did return to the base just before dawn.

✛ ✛ ✛

One nation, my nation — out of fear of being bombed by another nation — detonated close to one thousand nuclear warheads on — or, in, or over — its own land.

In *Regarding the Pain of Others,* Susan Sontag responds to a moment in *Three Guineas* where Virginia Woolf writes, "War is an abomination; a barbarity; war must be stopped." Sontag's response is a challenge in the guise of a question: "Who believes today that war can be abolished? No one, not even pacifists."

Fear of war has caused unalterable violence. The Bikini islanders forced to evacuate in 1946 to make way for Operation Crossroads — a series of nuclear tests the US military conducted to see what the effect of atomic explosions might be on warships — still cannot return. Inhabitants packed up their belongings and looked one last time at the topaz surf combing the shore. Commodore Ben H. Wyatt communicated with the islanders in a meeting that their evacuation would "help 'end all wars'." But even later that same year, there were worries about radiation contamination; in the early 1970s, residents were allowed to return, only to be evacuated from the islands again in 1978 due to radiation contamination.

The present is poisoned by the past in this region that had been governed by the UN but controlled by the US from 1948 to 1996 "as a de facto American colony." Old data feeds into calculations that spit out numbers that are supposed to provide information about radiation and exposure. But the numbers are much higher than expected. A recent article in Science News states:

> "Radioactive material such as cesium-137 currently produces, on average, 184 millirems of radiation per year on Bikini Atoll. And some parts of the island hit 639 millirems per year, researchers report online the week of June 6 in the Proceedings of the National Academy of Sciences. Those measurements, made last year, surpass the 100 millirems per year safety standard set by the United States and the Republic of the Marshall Islands, which controls the island."

What is important here is that the study *Science News* cites indicates that current radiation levels in the Bikini Atoll have been previously miscalculated due to old data and assumptions about what would happen to the radioactive material on the island over time. In depending on a false sense of the past, the present becomes even more dangerous.

✛ ✛ ✛

The Missile Park open to visitors inside the White Sands Missile Range displays over fifty missiles and rockets that had been part of tests on the site. One reminded me of a ship hull, the paint flaking off the tip. At the edge of my vision, I could see barbed wire, barracks, and flat lands that spread out into hills where rockets and bombs launch into the sky. The White Sands Missile Range Customer Handbook I found online promises that the site allows "visibility greater than 6 miles 311 days per year."

The day I visited, I couldn't tell if there had been a missile test. After I was "in the system," the man in the visitor center told me he was glad I arrived when I did, in the late afternoon, "so I could see things." He shook his head, "If you tried coming earlier … "

My eyes stung when I walked from the building to my car to drive through the gate. The air smelled like terracotta and eggs. I blinked. But the corners of my eyes still tingled. It was as though if I looked harder, turning my head, I could see more. See what I had come for. Instead, I walked around the warheads pointing up at the sky. Untethered from history.

I took my disposable camera out of my coat pocket to snap some pictures of the warheads. "Restricted Area" reads the sign you can spot from the access road. I realized this means that even sketching interpretations of what you see is not allowed.

After I slid the blocky plastic shape out of my coat pocket, I slid it back in.

I told a friend about what it was like to cross into the active missile test site, where off to the east, outside of vision, lies the detonation center of the world's first atomic explosion. We talked over Google Hangouts. My floating face spoke to her floating face. I felt my mouth losing language — my words becoming more and more vague the closer I got to the heart of the story.

When I told the computer screen floating with my friend's face about how I wanted to take some photos of the missiles, she disappeared. The screen went blank.

"Access denied," it said. The call wouldn't reconnect.

When she texted me, she said, "I think they're listening."

8. Front

The self must explore a thing until it screams. As a child, I would sit in the grass, touching the cold tufts with my fingers. *Dig, dig, dig.* I made a fist-sized hole. Inside it, a gray worm flipped over, curling like a question mark.

I would scream at the worm. I would scream at the hole I made. I would scream at what was inside it.

The self can be a receptacle.

The mouth takes everything in.

✝ ✝ ✝

Batman and I always joke about gunshots when firecrackers are launched in May, June, July, August, and September in our Chicago neighborhood on the west side.

Batman likes to walk me to the L when I'm leaving for an early flight at four a.m. He rolls my suitcase over the curb. Bump. Bump. At the exact moment when the wheels skipped concrete, we heard two gunshots explode the shadows from the trees.

With his arm, he barred me from moving forward. The echo came from a block away — the McDonald's parking lot. Sometimes, during gang initiation season, two men in white will chase a third man through the L cars. On the platform, I once saw two men try to push the third over the edge. This happened at rush hour in the morning.

I'd never really heard a gun go off like this: I've heard the stray shot of hunters in the forest when I played at my friend's house in the country. Those guns made me think of crows scaring off a roof. It frightened me still.

The sound is like your neighbor screaming at your friend in the backyard. Profane in its proximity to the swing set, your friend paling blank-faced as the wall of a warehouse.

It splits time for a second.

Batman and I paused, and so did a bicyclist coming home from somewhere — bartending? The sun would rise in two hours. He was about to cross the intersection in front of us, but he stopped and touched the toes of his Converse sneakers to the road. His bike made a clicking sound, and the wheels turned into the gravel of a pothole. We all looked around.

"Hey ... shit," I found myself saying. The bicyclist slowly started backing up his bike, still on his toes. Then he pedaled it out of there and disappeared.

"Let's go," said Batman.

I didn't want to go. I wanted to find out what was going on. "What happened?" I asked, not him, but the night, I suppose. I broke free of Batman's hold. Reason took over.

"It'll be too late to check this bag if we go around the block. I'm going to be late," I said.

I stepped toward the road and looked down it.

"No," said Batman.

My mind sometimes re-names places. Corner of Weed Wolf Graffiti Stickers. Pepsi Man's Curb. Daffodil Boulevard. One afternoon, after Batman and I had a minor argument — I wasn't sleeping well — I grabbed Charles Wright's *Zone Journals* off the shelf and took a walk: past the Grecian Statue, the Blue Corner, and Red Light Number 1. I joined the community of bums in the park between two roads. They were here a lot. Today, they were sharing a long yellow bottle. I decided to sit on a bench that faced away from the road. When I sat down, I noticed white graffiti arrows on the path that pointed at the seat. Oh well.

I opened my book. People walked their dogs through the grass. I wanted a dog. Then it caught my eye, a blocky white symbol. Someone had sprayed a different, frazzled purple symbol over it. I lined up my sandals with the arrow points. One, two. The symbols near them reminded me of when my little sister would copy my signature. The sunlight warmed my arms.

A man in a ripped T-shirt walked by, whistling. He slowed down.

I wondered if I had become part of a pattern of some kind. I had recently realized the apartment building on our corner was a major distribution center. The vans came on Thursdays. I would cross the street and then cross back. I was followed home once, but nothing happened. The two men, really young men, just watched me as I keyed into my apartment.

I stood up, stretching. My bench was the only one labeled with symbols.

✝ ✝ ✝

I'm touching a sheet of tulle threaded with gold plastic beads.

The cloth hangs above me. The cloth is deep purple, not quite plum. The room is lined with curtain displays. Like the one in front of me.

The curtains cover the perimeter of the room and also create alleys through it. I am standing at the farthest edge from the door. I like the plum one. It looks like a magician's curtain.

I put my face to the sheen.

A whisper of material. The creases still accordion-edged where the cloth had been folded inside its plastic packet. I think about putting my palms on the Corinthian columns of a museum.

Someone screams. A girl is standing by the front window.

Gunshots. Two.

Men's voices.

I slip behind the magic scrim.

I admire the cloth from inside of it. My back presses against the concrete wall behind me. The curtain is just opaque enough.

Men stamp through the aisles. Five or six, I would guess. I can see them even though I am layered outside of perception.

And now I can see them from above, as though I'm clinging to one of the curtain rods and looking straight down.

The curtain barely touches my mouth.

The curtain feels like the hair of someone sleeping next to you, strange, different, almost yours. It wakes me. My partner's hair brushes my mouth.

✛ ✛ ✛

There is actually such a thing as a cloak that removes you from time.

Batman explained this to me while he washed knives.

You can slip the cloak over your body and walk across a room.

You can stay inside the cloak as long as you like. When you slip into it, no one will see you. Then you will be seen again, reappearing next to the stove a breath later.

Your body is erased, zapped, swallowed by a hole.

The light will receive your body.

Then, your body will block the light, and you will re-enter the world.

✛ ✛ ✛

I'm touching a sheet of tulle threaded with gold plastic beads. The cloth hangs above me. My mother is touching another curtain next to this one, talking about how she would like to use it in a weaving she is making. She is an artist.

"I could do a lot with this," she says. Her glasses are pushed on top of her head.

"Why don't you get it?"

"It has to be juuust right ... " She inspects the hem.

Because my apartment doesn't yet have a shower curtain, or shower curtain rod, or window curtains, my mother thought we should check out Dollar Linen store on Milwaukee Avenue on our way back from the bakery. I love dollar stores. So does she. My family would buy Christmas gifts for each other at the dollar store next to the Aldi's when I was growing up.

Dollar Linen takes up two Chicago storefronts. Rugs hang in the window.

One half of the store, which could be a store in itself, is devoted to every possible household item. Drain plugs. Salad spinners. Juicers. Sets of picnic plates. And toys. Plastic doll heads that you can fit onto doll bodies. Feathered felt spiked with catnip. And toiletries. And cocoa butter. And candles of any scent. Candles with images of the Virgin Mary on them and prayers printed up the sides. My mother bought a Virgin Mary candle for me to burn.

When Batman and I first started seeing each other, back when we lived in Maryland, we walked from my apartment complex to the dollar store in the nearby strip mall in one of the DC suburbs. There we bought weird greeting cards for our mutual friend, who was driving to Georgia for her uncle's funeral. We laughed about how the cards said something a little wrong. We thought she'd laugh, too.

Congratulations! May your Riches Bring you Friendship.
Enjoy Retirement. You have the Rest of Your Life.
She liked the retirement card.

As we walked down the aisles, my mother and I ran our hands through robin's egg gauze, through butter yellow taffeta, through swaths of cotton spotted with cherries, and through lace tiebacks hanging up alone like ribbons lost from a dress.

On the way out the front door, she stopped at the cashier.

"You have a very nice place. What are your hours?" she asked.

"Thank you, Madam." With formality, the man handed us each a laminated business card. I could smell incense burning: cedar and raspberry. A man without teeth smiled at us and bowed his head as we crossed the threshold into the bright afternoon.

+ + +

The last time I went to Dollar Linen was because of a sign scrawled on the window:

We Cut Keys

It was winter.

"Hello. May I help you?"

It was the man who stood near the door. He wheezed.

"Do you sell cat food?" I asked.

I took off my mittens.

The man opened his mouth in surprise. The winter wind on his gums must cut to the nerve. I was wearing two pairs of pants and a hat under the hood of my coat.

"Cat food?" He stepped closer to me. "You don't want to get that here."

"Oh. OK."

He looked down at my mittens. One thumb was beginning to unravel.

"Do you have drain traps?"

"Yes, yes. Follow me, Madam."

This store had *everything*. Roach traps in S, M, L. Hand towels dyed in red spots: prints that tomatoes make when hurled at a garage. The man led me down one of the aisles along the room's edge. I could hear my boots scuffing the linoleum floor. There were no sounds, not even the radio. If I were by myself, I would have cut straight down the center of the room. The back door was in the center of the room.

I thought of my body cutting through the air.

Some guys appeared: They sauntered toward us.

"Thanks." The man's eyes were red.

"Good day, sir," responded my guide. He turned to me. "This?" he asked me and pointed to a series of hooks.

There were four different drain traps hanging on the wall. We were in the back of the room.

I felt warm and unzipped my coat. I loosened the scarf at my throat, and chose two traps (one was $1.00, and the other $1.75).

Then, my guide led me to the front, where I could smell the incense. I put the traps on the cashier's counter. I asked about having some keys cut. The cashier took my key ring from my hands and marked the two I wanted copied with a Sharpie. I didn't like that. He turned away, and the machine began.

In the machine, my keys made a shrill, grinding noise: it reminded me of that sound of bones being run through a wood-chipper in the movie *Fargo*.

"It sure is cold out," I said.

"Yes, yes."

The machine ground and ground.

"But it is nice and warm in here!" I said. I don't know why I said that.

The man without teeth walked briskly toward the door. A kid walked in. The kid was wearing a puffy Blackhawks coat that touched his knees. He must have been twelve, and in his older brother's jacket. Or, maybe it had always been his. The toothless man was happy to see him. They shook hands and laughed.

The child's skin was pocked. His eyes were red. The two of them disappeared for a moment, and when they reappeared the boy was putting something into his pocket. I stared, and the cashier caught me.

"Yes, it's warm. My poor heating bill!" he said in mock good humor. But his were eyes sharp as he looked up at me from his work.

"Oh, yes! I can only imagine!" I sung. The shriek of the key-cutter cut out just as I began to speak. "Heat is so expensive these days."

It was like I was projecting to an empty theatre.

For a moment, the cashier held up both sets of my keys: the thicker, copper-colored ones my landlord handed me in August, and the shiny new gold ones.

His fingertips played with the new keys, the ones he made, showing the metal to the light.

I remembered the men that kept coming to the front of the store from a room in the back. I noticed I was the only woman there. I noticed no one else was buying anything. I realized there was always a man on lookout at the front door. I thought about how the plastic cups, the dolls, the candy, all of it looked old: some of it dusty. I thought about my comment, about the heat. How did Dollar Linen pay to heat the building? I remembered the men that kept coming to the front of the store from a room in the back.

I looked around. The cashier watched me look around.

Get out, a voice said. It wasn't my voice, but it was inside me.

It's the voice that said *Stand up* when two men sat, one in front and one next to me, on an empty train car of the DC metro.

Sometimes the voice has a form. It pushes you, gently, to the door of the train and onto the platform when you need to go. There is a shift in atmosphere, and you feel the gentle push on your back. *Back up.*

Stop digging at it. The thing. Stop thinking about it, wondering about it. See the hole? Stop it. You will dig something up. You will dig up the thing that exists out of sight. The thing that coils around the roots of it all.

The Midwestern sky sometimes stripes with clouds so high that it feels like we are inside a giant bowl.

It is headache bright.

One day, the sky will be just like this: glaucoma blue.

Listen. You might not believe it, but there is such a thing as a scrim. One day you will rip it.

You will fight against the hands pushing you to walk away. Goodbye, Batman. You'll take a shortcut.

The sky — I want to say it will rip, too. That the epiphany will dissolve. That there won't be one. That the shadows aren't already making lace of your arms.

9. Afterimage (III)

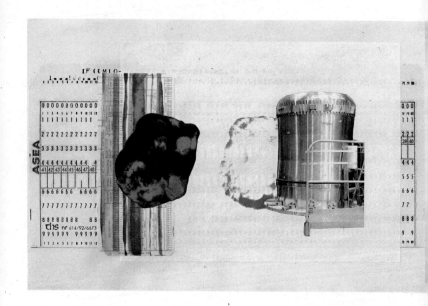

A mistake. On mistakes. I discovered the stain by accident. I had been saturating the cap of the mushroom cloud with the tip of a Prisma-color marker. Underneath the page, I opened my writing notebook — which is a sketch-book — to protect the drafting table from stray marks. The table was not mine. I worked in a blue cabin in the woods. I lifted the wet cloud shape, and underneath, the same shape bled into my notebook. Radiation bleeds into the air and soil. I can't remember if the scrap of a poem scribbled that morning floated above or beneath. I cut it out. You can see the punch card background through this stained page. Numbers through my notebook. The metal canister, through which the stain emerges, holds radioactive material.

10. Gone

The CDC was supposed to issue a briefing about how the public might prepare for a nuclear attack. This briefing appeared suddenly during the increased tension between North Korea and the US in 2018. Shortly after this briefing, at the time of my writing this, the "Public Health Response to a Nuclear Detonation" link for the CDC that had been showing up in my Google search changed to a page called "Public Health Response to Severe Influenza" when you click on it. An epigraph for the new title says the following:

"Note: CDC Public Health Grand Rounds topic change to: 'Public Health Response to Severe Influenza'."

However, there isn't language about "nuclear" or "detonation" anywhere on the site. There is a note that says this: "Note: The previous public health topic will be rescheduled for a future Grand Rounds."

Rescheduled for a future. Note: Not the now. A future now. Note: I hope that this future now, in reality, stays that way. Even though I'm horrified that information about how to deal with a catastrophic event has been erased. Note: That is what a word like *this* is for. To hold something in place.

I imagine sending my hope that we will never need a warning like this one up into the air from my cupped hands. It would lift off, birdlike, and so easy to imagine, passing from my skin to my eyes then above me to the tops of the trees — the trees of my part-Midwestern childhood, sugar maple so much like fire in the fall — and into the sky marbled with cirrus clouds. When my sister was born, I remember standing with my father and brother in the front yard and releasing a balloon. I felt such sadness as it passed above the highest tips of the brittle leaves, so delicate in the wind.

Open your mouth, and inside I will put a dollop of cream. Isn't it better than a cold knife on the tongue, pressed there like a medieval tool? *Which tool?* a friend would ask. I'd answer, *A scythe.* Did you know children would be sent into the fields with bells to scare birds away from the seeds? Running between the rows in the dirt and swinging the clapper into the lip. Away, away, the swallows scattered, taking death in their wings.

When I lost my second pregnancy, after losing the first, I believed I saw my child in the reservoir. Batman and I had hiked there once via the "interpretive trail," which on the map looks like a loop but in reality takes you along the water to a dead end at the edge of a cliff. Batman, convinced we could leap down the steep slope and cling to the trunks of trees on the way, tried to lead me. Cape-like shadows pulled behind him. I only made it a few steps down before climbing out; we had to double back, our feet finding our shoeprints in the dusty soil of the trail. This time, we had started the path in the high grasses and stayed there. Water below. The townspeople of Santa Fe once believed this small reservoir would be a main source of drinking water. Home to songbirds. One hundred and forty kinds. Silvery brown wings. *Full-throated ease.* The little heartbeat that had stopped. The face I had seen on a screen. Too early to know, but when I saw it then, I knew. *Him. Goodbye, goodbye,* I said, and we stayed by the water watching the light warp it.

11. Afterimage (IV)

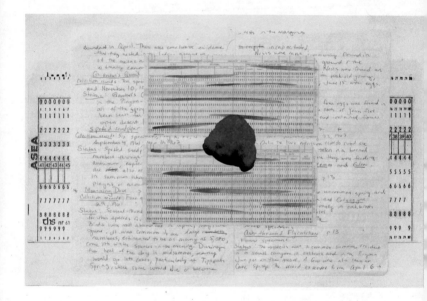

This work was hard for me to make, stroking the pigment over the card, letting it soak in slowly. My hand moved the brush quickly across the paper, and I had to leave the bold marks alone. I painted horizon lines — blue streaks of water — over the computer punch cards. These lines show a total commitment to decisions. They show a steady hand. Steer the ship through the waves. Imagine birds dipping into water.

There are places on this earth that look pristine, cerulean. Sky in the water. A living ruin.

Wind combed. Birds migrate through these areas, and in the desert. Pausing in scorched brush. Feeding off of berries washed in contaminants. Flying off, somewhere else.

12. Afterimage (V)

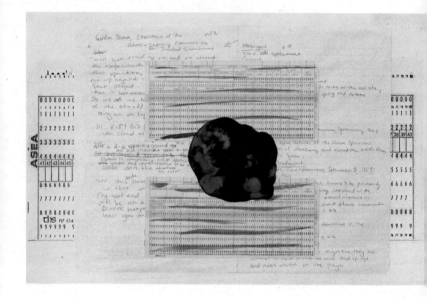

Well, you could go on and on about —

— Gordon Dean, Atomic Energy Commission, 1952

Water dark blue in color

                          fission weapon
the cloud

                              this
operation
            the next
                    each project
                        leave you
                        ~~*who*~~

13. Afterimage (V): Description Attempt

In *Afterimage (V)*, on the left side, you can see a partial transcript of one of the declassified nuclear test films I watched over and over. Particularly, this language comes from a film depicting the explosion and aftermath of "Ivy Mike," a massive hydrogen bomb test — the first thermonuclear device ever detonated — that the US set off in the Marshall Islands in 1952. On the right side, you'll see a page from my notebook where I made notes of information from *Birds of the Nevada Test Site*, published in the Brigham Young University Science Bulletin's Biological Series (Volume III, Number 1) in June 1963.

What the viewer can glimpse in my partially scribbled hand-writing is information about the house sparrow and meadowlark while these birds migrated around and through sites where the US detonated nuclear devices in the 1960s. In *Afterimage (V)*, the green atomic cloud swirls in the center, water-like. I'm reminded of the color of algae blooms photographed from space. On the page, the cloud looks like a hole to me, something that could suck everything in. The computer punch cards dashed with blue brushstrokes underneath the atomic cloud are meant to evoke water. As I painted them, I wanted to emphasize the gestural potential of the line and for it to interact with the punch cards underneath, which were meant to record employee hours. Perhaps in articulating a seascape in this context, I could invite a meditation on the labor that went into the nuclear material and device that exploded the "Ivy Mike" bomb. Maybe my engagement with these disparate materials could invite a reader to look deeply at them, to think about them, and also to let the eye move over the page.

These works, all of the *Afterimage* collages in the series, are visual expressions of my own journey through archival materials. When I touch the punched holes of the Fortran cards, I wonder at how to read them. The multi-colored brain-like clouds reflect my journey through my notes about the ways these tests touched nature's cyclical patterns and our human attempt to understand and regard the destruction they wrought. The curls and scribbles copy notes recorded about the wildlife that migrated through the atomic desert. My handwriting also loops around words scientists uttered before the bombs decimated communities in the Marshall Islands. The bombs they built and chose to detonate, eradicating the homeland for the Marshall Islanders who were promised they could return.

14. Afterimage (VI)

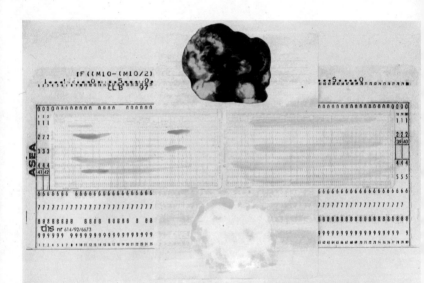

Stain as echo

as mirror

as residue

The bulb glows

marks your eyes

your eyelids

closed

closed

15. Stain

As I saturate the atomic clouds with color, which began as a way for me to engage my hand and my brain with the shapes inside those boiling, terrible images, the blooms begin soaking into the notebook paper I placed underneath them to protect the drafting table. (Have I said this? I have said this.) When I lift the page I had been soaking, I see a kind of afterimage — another repetition.

16. Afterimage (VII)

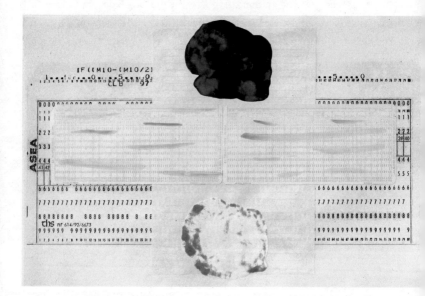

In my cabin in the woods, I could hear rain droplets beating on the ferns that bowed outside my window.

I wanted to paint a lush, green horizon.

How could I invite a viewer to think about the visual impression of something so terrible, so deeply imprinted into our collective consciousness that we don't want to see it?

The studio had windows on three sides that glowed green. After living in the high desert of Northern New Mexico, I had become acclimated to a palette of browns and pinks. I touched the cool screens. Smelled the wet earth.

The forest floor seemed to move like water catching the light.

17. Work

I slide the computer punch cards from their mailing envelopes and fan them out on my desk. I paint over a few of the cards with watercolor stains, washing the "isotopes" columns and the "enrich (%)" columns with color. I wash the "employee number," "hours" and "money" columns. I washed "net change." I will let these few cards dry and put them back in their envelopes with the other cards.

Earlier, on residency, I brought photocopies of the 8x10s — which an archivist had given me — to Staples. (Have I said this? I have said this.) I acquired these images on a snowy January day when I went to the Palace of the Governors Photo Archives in Santa Fe. An archivist there gave them to me. The 8x10s were prints of the very first photographs taken of a nuclear explosion: the Trinity Test detonated near Alamogordo, New Mexico, on July 16, 1945.

These images troubled me with their almost incomprehensible shadows. The more I looked, the more I thought I would see. So I would stare.

Like now, paintbrush in hand. Marker uncapped.

18. Afterimage (VIII)

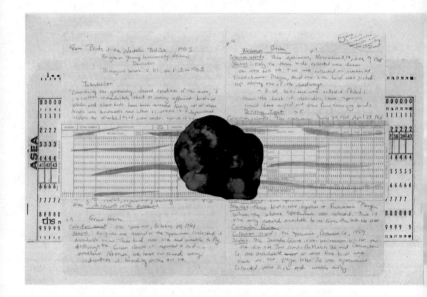

Migrating birds taking the radioactive materials across the country with them?

My note, circled in the top corner of my notebook, asks a question about diffusion.

Wings. I wanted the water-like brushstrokes to spread out from the teal spot and suck everything into it as though the form itself could fly off with itself.

19. Body

Monday, and children were walking through the streets, plastic packs
on their backs like oxygen tanks for the Moon, and pickup trucks —
Fords and Chevys — lingered bumper to bumper outside the police
station and looped around the plaza with its white gazebo and statue
of the Virgin,

   and the sun looked like liquid, and the road leading away that
bridged the river's slush of mud and Doritos bags became a TV set
— yellow tape, film crew, a sheriff in a Stetson — and that's what I
thought when I saw the barricades, and that's what a friend thought
because the TV show staging our town to be Wyoming wanted to use
his front door,

   and in the café, I sat at the wood table on a chair with legs uneven as a teenager's jeans and rocked side-to-side like I was riding in
an old van when the children suddenly flooded in, their voices quick
in the afternoon air like little bells,

   and they shouted each other's names and tried to laugh out the
dark that was beginning to shimmer almost green in the windows
with a luster I can't describe, the changing light cuing something
about to fly off the stage of the world like deck umbrellas no one
remembered to bring in before a hurricane, but there are no hurricanes
here, and then a word began echoing in the room, all around me,
beginning in the mouths of the children and easing into noise, a garble
of gossip,

approaching like a snake you hardly hear gliding over gravel,

but its presence made us look at each other differently,
peripherally, and I found myself thinking of *never* and wanting to
construct lies with it, like *I never stood by a creek and watched
water glass the sky,* and *I was never as young as that table of kids,*
their cheeks flushed pink with sugar,

and the rumor suddenly wore its vowels and consonants loudly,
body, the children said, *body,* and then I heard parents say, *body in the
back of a pickup truck,* and then *parked on the street out there,* then
dead, dead, driven down from the mountains, the state called in, *body*
killed up by the hot springs, killed up by the community college,

dumped at night in the pickup bed and driven into town as
though for a parade, and someone did this, lives here, shot the body
in the head, or slit the throat with a kitchen knife, and I could see the
truck through the window, person gone, the bed that carried it lifted
up on a hook and chain, the vehicle almost a persona of a vehicle,
and I thought about how evidence can seem like a curtain pulled shut
in a window,

and outside, on the corner, a grassroots journalist talked at the
screen of her phone about *disappeared women,* how many there are,
how mothers and sisters order T-shirts printed with birthday and
yearbook photos of them smiling and wear the dead over the ribs and
chest and lungs (mothers and sisters and cousins march in the fiesta

parade chanting *justice*), but later I heard that the body belonged to a man, a man my friend's coworker's neighbor knew, and the paper did not give a name, just *body*, and *individual*, the language of free enterprise, and at the edge of it all, someone read *body* and watched the sun rise — this time no bones in the ground — and thought, *how easy it was*.

20. Afterimage (IX)

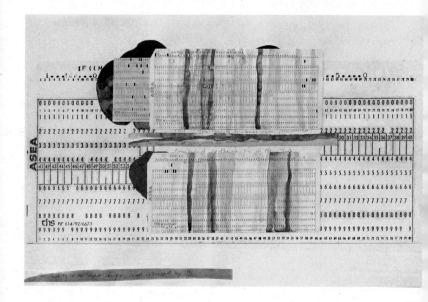

A meditation on color, the browns of the Southwest. And also blood.

Dripping down, rust in water, calcifying.

Sometimes, you think you see rain, but it doesn't reach the dirt. A column stretches down from the clouds and vanishes.

The reality of the object, therefore, is not exhausted by its —

I jotted this down from a book on architecture with a yellow cover I borrowed from the residency library. I wrote the title down, somewhere, but as this language has been ripped from its context, I will tear this fragment further from its source. *Reality [ ] is not exhausted —*

Compared to the skyline of New York

This is the largest fireball ever produced

III.

21. Lions and Pigeons

NYC

All I needed was a library card to access the books on military history. The Stephen A. Schwartzman Building of the New York Public Library on 42nd Street belongs to the city of New York. So a metro card, a library card (which I obtained showing proof of residency in NYC), and here I am, transported from my kitchen and its crumbs to Manhattan, after chaperoning my toddler with hands sticky from breakfast to her camp. Then the subway and its thick, July heat. Then the marble steps up to the Main Branch. Flanking the steps are stone lions. Flocks of pigeons beat their wings over their staged ferocity. Here are predators with symbolic birds of peace flapping around their manes, landing, and then picking at hotdog buns and potato chips scattered in Bryant Park adjacent to the massive building.

If I can't hunt down the information I need, studying footnotes and bibliographies, reading the shadows and empty spaces, will I, too, end up picking at crumbs?

At the playground in the afternoon, after I dash back to the subway and jog to the pick-up door for my toddler's camp a few blocks from my apartment, I'll craft cakes and build towers in the sand, teach her to share with the boy from camp she recognizes at the playground. What is hers is hers in the wet sand: broken yellow excavators with missing wheels, yogurt cups cracked at the edges, and a single pink shovel. Artifacts from previous seasons, previous children, who keep burying, finding, and reburying these remnants of prior games.

The air is hazy, the city on a summer schedule. Sleepy. Midafternoon, I'm at the playground with nannies, grandmothers, and some parents, but not many. My hours teaching, freelancing, and writing are odd, scattered, rise sometimes with the moon. I take off my socks and wet my feet in the cold puddle pooling between the rubber squares under the play gym and the fountain. I let my daughter splash my calves.

"Do you work?" a grandmother asks me. She comes in from Queens three times a week to watch her daughter's children. *Eagle radar. Kadena Air Base. Okinawa.* Facts stir in my brain while I try to hold up a conversation, my mind split between research and parenting. I'd sprinted from the subway station to the pick-up line, and I felt like I was still at the library.

I say, "I work," and begin explaining. And I pick up the child, drop her off, wipe her mouth, pack snacks, schedule playdates, soothe bruises. And there is an overdue interview, an upcoming podcast, student emails. The work interwoven, parenting, teaching, and writing. A delicate balance. A nanny recently scolded me for letting my daughter wear her sneakers on her wrong feet. "She put them on herself," I explained. "I'm so proud!" I could see the eyeroll. Sometimes, I'm mistaken for a sitter or a nanny. A sitter will talk to me, and then realize I'm the parent and laugh with embarrassment after they've disclosed things about their employer. Notebook in a canvas bag bumping my hip, I've caught toddlers falling backward off ladders, handed them chalk, kept them from wandering out the playground gate. Once I dashed out and caught a kid who bolted for the busy street.

Writing *is* work, but not in the capitalistic maw that pulps all things that don't stuff the market. The maw that can erase artmaking, writing, parenting. Certain kinds of teaching. The city churns, glass reflecting light, steel beams extending to the sky. Old homes become chopped up into smaller and smaller apartments.

Parenting *is* work. This is not a new statement, but it needs to be said again and again.

A parent emailed me to invite me to take my child and her child with her child's nanny to a "bubble party" in the park on Friday at three p.m. There was a clown. I wasn't teaching that day, so I said yes. There were gigantic wands. We chased the warping blobs of soap lifting off from their dripping nets into the air above the grass. Observed the bubbles rise skyward then collapse as though in slow motion into strings of viscous fluid.

Our hands, outstretched, empty, but wanting more.

Not wanting to be clean. Wanting to hold the impossible.

We waited to catch the shape of the light, looking for the spaces around where the bubble once glimmered.

✢ ✢ ✢

Outside the Main Branch on 42nd Street, I watch pigeons cast quick shadows over the lion's mouth before dashing up the steps. Crumbs on the stones. The truth caught in the shapes that move, in the indiscernible edge between what is and what is not.

Who you are and who you are not.

What is and what is not.

22. Bats and Cats

I've disliked bats my whole life. So choosing to call my spouse Batman here might be an odd choice. In my eyes, he can switch into superhero mode — making choices as swiftly as leaping off a skyscraper — while doing so wordlessly, effortlessly. I tend to obsess over things. Agonize over organizing a countertop. Maybe because I'm Bi and with a man, I've decided to make him Batman. Appearing from the shadows. Allowing me to be both here and there. Although unlike Bruce Wayne, who has inexhaustible wealth, my Batman was the youngest of eleven children. Together, we maxed out credit cards. We squeezed lemons into watery beer while we sweated in front of a box fan. We rode the train at one a.m. instead of paying for a cab. And he watched me go, from time to time, and return.

When my cat of seventeen years died at home at the old age of twenty, Batman appeared from the shadows, wrapping her in a white towel and tucking her brindled paws underneath her before rigor mortis set in. I was out of town, doing research in Santa Fe. He called three emergency clinics and then found a cremation service that will drive to your apartment in NYC, collect your animal, and say something kind to you, returning her in a little box with a brass nameplate. Half a country away, I was distraught. He told me she waited until I was away to die to spare me, that she was ready, which comforted me.

+ + +

During the day, in a number of apartments we've shared, a crumpled brown bat has latched onto the outside of our window or just outside our door to sleep in the cool penumbra of a shadow. When bats sleep, they are so still. And when they fly, they swoop soundlessly — yes, sometimes brushing against your shoulders and tapping the top of your head with leathery wings.

+ + +

After I gave birth to our daughter in New Mexico, a friend visited me during the difficult weeks I felt like I couldn't leave the apartment. Our infant had almost died after she was born because of poor care she received for a tongue-tie release. A pediatric dentist swabbed numbing gel into her mouth. She choked afterward, turning as blue as death.

Dying, eyes wide in terror.

I saved her life, somehow. I noticed she wasn't breathing in her car seat and pulled her out, pulling strings of goo out of her mouth. I flipped her and did the exact maneuver I had practiced on a vinyl-headed and cloth-bodied baby doll in a birthing class weeks before. (A class I almost forgot to register for, almost didn't take.) Enough goo and milk and pus came out that the infant sputtered and screamed.

She almost died. And didn't.

I will never forget watching her begin the journey backwards, from birth to death.

And so, after that when she slept, I thought she was dead.

When I held her, I thought she was dead.

She looked like a doll to me, in my arms.

I watched the moon rise from the window and the stars collect in the desert sky.

All of this looked like the afterlife. My life. Her life. I was dead, and she was dead, and we did not exist in the world any longer. And I was afraid to leave the apartment with this infant-doll. So my friend's visit was a gift. Another human! A writer! A reader! We talked about books! She brought fried plantains and guacamole! I forgot I was holding a doll that was my baby that was alive but almost wasn't and that I had to keep checking on to make sure she was breathing.

My friend and I talked about the bat napping upside down outside. We watched Christine Blasey Ford's testimony against Brett Kavanaugh and believed her with our whole hearts. And we still believed in a world where her words would matter enough to prevent his confirmation, even though we knew he would be sworn in anyway.

"Bats love their babies!" my friend reminded me after I ranted about how much I dislike bats. Before she arrived, I'd texted her to be careful at the door not to wake the sleeping bat. I didn't know if it would wake up and bite her. Would it? Or would it remain upside-down and watch her, eyes open?

After my friend left, I rethought the bat outside the door. Maybe she slept deeply, waiting to give birth to her pup.

Maybe she'd eaten the eggs from the nearby starling nest to nourish herself.

+ + +

Batman brought us to NYC, to Gotham City, from the desert. Batman was a good father already, endlessly patient. And he helped me see that I could do it, that I could be the mother to my child — my very much alive child.

+ + +

If Batman is my partner-in-crime, am I Catwoman? If so, my claws and ears mean more than a cat suit. (Though I'm all for a sexy cat suit.) My ears tingle when information is absent, when something isn't said. I protract my claws and wait, ready to pounce. My feet might land quietly from a ledge, but they land.

+ + +

When my cat died shortly after her twentieth birthday, I felt like a part of me died, too — that part she knew and protected, all the most foolish years of my life when I was in my early twenties. How she followed me from room to room. Comforted me. And then, a few years before her death, she would dart across the room and leap on my lap at three a.m., when I could finally get my daughter to sleep.

In the only dream I had of her after my cat died, she sat on my lap and then spoke. She said, *It was hard to find you. But I found you.*

23. Ghost

Each day, the maple tree outside the window becomes thicker, leaf growing into leaf. The sun collects in ridged pockets that the branches gently ruffle. Yet the thin branches remain still — a young green maple. A new apartment. Same neighborhood in the unceded homeland of the Lenape people. I think about this violence daily.

Boxes still stacked by windows. But light, actual light, falls onto the floor. I stretch out on my bed after another night hardly sleeping. My daughter insisted on being carried all the way to preschool along with her enormous frog umbrella and backpack (she wouldn't sit in the stroller or walk with me). But she did wear the polka dot COVID mask required by her school over her ticklish nose and open lips that print a wet O into the fabric. So I will *focus on the positives,* as the Instagram parenting account tells me with a brief video. *Positive* is now a negative word in my mind, though, since fear of testing positive brings dread.

Now, among the pile of sweaters I need to sort through and the freelance checks I cashed and didn't shred before the move (my signature on the rectangular slips of paper stuffed in boxes with seven-year-old diaries and broken costume jewelry from a great-aunt or a thrift store), I think to myself it is time to try again. Discard what tugs on me from the past. Make room for the air, the light. Try to be a full person: or, how I think a full person lives. A person who sleeps seven hours, keeps an accurate calendar, and sorts through boxes instead of moving them from place to place untouched.

But I also need to finish the book. This book.

I did *promise* to finish. I've told people I am finishing it. Shoving my imposter syndrome into another box — a box always with more room in the corners. I would use the cash from a grant to pay for some summer childcare (though I didn't say that was what the money was for, exactly, in my grant proposal) to visit the New York Public Library and begin working with texts in the military archives that are held in the mysterious vault under 5th Avenue and 42nd Street's blur of taxis and buses where pigeons flap loudly over the fountain and scatter through the uneven metal chairs in Bryant Park. The funds helped me purchase a new laptop, as my old one would pause while I typed, holding my words in ransom over a blank line on the Word document until better ideas materialized. (And when the better ideas appeared, the old words finally settled like moss-fuzzed blackberries I wanted to savor but had to trash.)

But the big expense that my grant proposal detailed would be a trip for me to visit ground zero of the Trinity atomic blast crater one of the two weekends a year that the US Military opened the site to civilians.

Nestled in the Chihuahuan Desert of New Mexico and still radioactive, yet safe to visit briefly — as safe as an international flight — Trinity Site is where J. Robert Oppenheimer and General Leslie Groves peered into the crater at the twisted remains of the bomb tower and marveled at what they had done.

And I do not want to go.

When I lived in New Mexico, I had been trying to become pregnant, or was pregnant, for four years, so I never made the less-far-than-you'd-think drive from Santa Fe to the access road to the north entry to the site the first weekend in October or April. I didn't want to bring the cells I sometimes grew or hoped to grow to a nuclear test site.

I gave a reading at Oklahoma State University in February 2020, a few weeks before New York City went into lockdown — that odd time when we sanitized our hands and sat together on trains and on planes. One woman in a pale blue surgical mask sat next to me on the American Airlines flight from JFK to Stillwater via Dallas joking about her covered mouth to a voiceless and faceless person on the other end of her cell phone as the rest of us sat unmasked and cupping hand sanitizer into our open palms. After my reading, during that strange month before we knew lockdown would be our reality, an inquisitive audience member raised his hand. My daughter was just over one year old. At that time, I still pumped milk from my breasts in the bathroom when I travelled and dumped it down the sink when I couldn't store it and bring it home. As I called on the questioner, feeling my nipples tingle with milk, I remember regarding the whole room — all of the graduate students, the university newspaper photographer, and the donors who funded my visit. We had just shared green chili and chicken enchiladas at the program director's home. *New York — you won't get these skies there,* said one of the donors. *Or this chili,* I added. I genuinely missed the bluebell sky, the landscape that extended for miles and miles. And yes, the chili. I love the Southwest.

But after this dinner, after my talk, the man, a young faculty member, asked, *Well, why didn't you just go to the Trinity blast site when you lived there, since you went to the White Sands Missile Range?* At that point, I hadn't any plan to visit the blast crater.

His question echoed in the oak-paneled room, and among the pews: the hall was also a church. I felt like I had been standing at the pulpit.

In that moment, I felt like I was the minister and one of my congregants interrupted the service to asked me why I didn't believe in God. Or the Godhead site. The Trinity Site. Why not go to the place where all and nothing have been made. Where all could have been taken away.

I panicked.

At the time, I took a deep breath and somehow calmly asserted that what was interesting to me was not necessarily the spectacle of the crater on a day curated by the US Military, but what it would mean to visit the site on an "ordinary" day. A day that the military complex wasn't expecting carloads of atomic tourists. A day that other kinds of weapons may or may not be tested, access may or may not be denied to even the edge where the missile museum is located. And that I had already done this — visited the Warhead Museum on the White Sands Missile Range on a weekday the first January I lived in the Southwest.

But after the talk, when he approached me to bring up the question again, because he had been there himself (and lived in New Mexico at one point, which helped me understand that his question wasn't intended to pull the lynchpin out of my research), I did say, *I had been trying to conceive for four years. I didn't want to go to a known radioactive site while I was pregnant.*

He murmured something apologetic.

Such is the delicate dance of having one kind of body in an academic space.

But I keep thinking about how fortunate I was to be able to make this choice *not* to go to the test site at that time, not to live extremely close to point of the earth blasted open into poison even though the entire state has been impacted by this nuclear history.

✢ ✢ ✢

Now that I am a mother, I find myself disoriented even further about this upcoming trip, this research. I still don't want to go to the Trinity bomb crater, even though I wrote a budget specifically to fund the trip. The radiation I will absorb would be so minimal — less than the flight itself out there, I reread and say again here — but all the same, now that I had split open, bled out, and released a pair of lungs into the world with a heart that murmurs and skips, with a voice that asks, *Why don't you try?* when I say something cannot be done, I worry about contaminating her while contaminating myself.

What will the research trip to the radioactive site mean to her, if anything? *What if I get sick?*, the question parents have been asking themselves during the pandemic, rises in my throat.

But *Why don't you try?* is what she asks when I stumble on a step while she slides off of my hip and I have to set her down. *Why don't you try?* when I can't reach a glass jar she wants from the counter. *Why don't you try?* when the linden leaf in my fingers flies out of my hand and into a sunny pile of leaves that all look the same to me. *Find it.*

Try, try, her little voice urges.

When knees and elbows inside of me pushed on my skin and my ribs, she was *not there* yet, but to me was also *here*. She still feels *here*, inside, now that she is on the outside.

She had known the inside. The timeless darkness where one of my body's creative forces comes from.

And I had taken her, as a small creature-not-yet-here on the inside, *not there*, to Los Alamos, the town housing the laboratory that first designed nuclear weapons and now holds them, keeps them ready for use. Children are born there. People live there. Going there pregnant isn't a risk.

But the idea of visiting the atomic blast crater that marked the world's descent into the Anthropocene — which fingerprinted all we know with our rough skin, our greed — while my own body was creating life was not something I could do. My feet would not press into the soil that has been through the trauma of how we could create nothing from something and take away the world.

Her growing-into-life heart had been to Monument Valley on the Navajo Nation where I watched rain slash the red stone Three Sisters and ponies drink from a tire tread puddle. After observing the red wind-carved monuments, I ate soft fry bread in the visitor center while flat clouds hovered over the brick-colored dirt. And I learned about the uranium mines from a wall display. *Navajo mines.* I was on Diné land, but I did not read about the history of mining before my visit. Since the 1940s, when white colonialists opened up the earth in pockets all over the sacred land for the yellow cake dust, rivulets in the rock have bled poison. Mothers drank it, bathed infants in the water. After the rain stopped, when the being inside of me slept, I stepped outside and smelled the petrichor — the earth. It smelled like dirt and blood. I held up my hand and it looked like the same size as the mitten butte in the distance.

At two, my child remembered being inside me. *The big big beat* of my heart. All the blue of the veiny purse she touched. The *special song* she sang while opening and closing her mouth.

Then she forgot.

The uranium mines seem everywhere and nowhere. They are around, nearby, but not easy to locate. This vagueness is reassuring if you buy the story — the forgetting. Later, I read that the sand-like waste from some of the mines appeared in children's playgrounds on the Navajo Nation. And the unsealed tunnels, unsealed pits —

Abandoned dangers.

I correct myself. In February 2021, the EPA announced that three corporations would be contracted to clean up the mines. And so, now I can easily locate a map of these mines and see a dense cluster of red dots all over Monument Valley. Some of the dots overlap one another and look like stacked poker chips. After my trip to Monument Valley when I became aware of the history, I now acknowledge my own lack of knowledge about the full extent of mining on Diné land.

I had taken for granted that, as a tourist, I would take in the beauty and mystery of Monument Valley Tribal Park (Tsé Bii' Ndzisgaii) as a visitor who could enter and leave, unharming the landscape that whiteness had drilled into, lied about, and left scarred.

And I had taken for granted also what it means to wonder even now, after my daughter is in the world and picking up crushed lilacs from the sidewalk, what the effect might have been on her in my womb when the US Government left exposed mines near homes where children could play, mines I didn't go near at Monument Valley that rainy visit.

✢ ✢ ✢

The word *granted* makes me think of the word "grant." An agreement, an assumption of truth. I think about how Indigenous communities forced to relocate were given land grants by the US government. I think about the sorrow that American dirt and soil has held and continues to hold. And the wildflowers and grasses that peek out of cracked soil, somehow.

Even in planning to visit the place where my grandfather flew planes and drove a jeep labeled with the 316th bomb wing under skies blue as the American flag, I doubt that the military site itself will give me a glimpse of what my grandfather witnessed. Yet I am pulled there.

I know the place itself will tell me something. But what?

✢ ✢ ✢

I keep thinking I need to check all of the things I said I would do off of my list before rolling up my sleeves and finishing this book. Sometimes mapping out a plan, wrestling with a subject — that can be important work, too. I look at potential flights to New Mexico for

October, pricing them, wondering where to stay. I'm tempted to stay in the town of Truth or Consequences. The town of Hot Springs changed its name to Truth or Consequences so that the game show, *Truth or Consequences,* would host one episode there. The big tenth anniversary episode. Now the town lives with the legacy of this name. And the game show does not hold a place in our mouths.

Albuquerque is much closer to the entrance gate to the atomic blast crater, so I decide to stay there instead. Closer to the actual truth, the actual consequences.

The first weekend in October, when the tree outside my new apartment will crinkle into red leaves and my coat gets wet in the morning mist, I will go to JFK or LaGuardia, board a plane, land somewhere in Texas, board another plane, and land in Albuquerque.

Will I feel like a mother slipping out of the robe of motherhood? Will my daughter finally, once and for all, wean? My mind plays out what I will experience, as though imagining the trip is the same as being there. Something about the way I've been connecting with the world and other people for so many months, over a year at this point in the pandemic, by peering into my laptop screen makes me think that if I look at photos, recall my past experiences, and read enough about each individual step of my journey, imagining going will be the same as actually pressing my boots into the soil.

The air will smell dry and sweet when I exit the airport and take the shuttle to the car rental lot. The sun will blare off the other vehicles, vectoring into little stars, if I arrive in daylight. If not, the moon will cast a clear-cut shadow. Moonlight in New Mexico can be blue, startlingly bright, I remember.

I'll take the car keys, hope as I sit in the hot seat that the fuel filter isn't clogged so my foot won't shove the pedal to the car floor as I edge around cliffs and drive out into the desert.

I imagine joining the other tourists who have decided to journey to the origin site of the Anthropocene. But I can't envision them with my mind's eye — all I see is a blurred crowd.

But we'll go where scientists wondered if they'd set the earth's atmosphere on fire. And set off the explosion anyway. I know cars will line up at the checkpoint, IDs will be reviewed. I can't think about what this will feel like, what I will learn from it. All I know is that we will be led through the weapons test site to the inaccessible place. A place almost blotted out. A place forbidden. A memory hidden.

I feel like I can write about this experience without traveling there. But traveling there means more than the story of the trip. Putting your body in the place where total disaster set loose a storm of dirt and glass — there is no way to understand what this means until your feet have touched it.

All was lost there: someone saw the tower of smoke shooting up to heaven and thought that this could be duplicated, triplicated. And more, and more.

That kind of greed is monstrous, yes. The darkness after the light sucked into the throats and ears of the men in power, particularly General Leslie Groves. After the world learned about what the US did with nuclear weapons in Japan, Groves spoke to his officers. "It is not an inhuman weapon," he said to them. The exact opposite of the truth.

When kids are arguing at the playground, an adult steps in. "I don't care who started it. You need to stop fighting," is the typical response. Not *you started it so you deserve this*.

Gen. Groves had said, "I think our best answer to anyone who doubts this is that we did not start the war and if they don't like the way that we ended it, to remember that they started."

One place on earth holds the beginning of the end. It holds the beginning of the interplay between infinite power and infinite destruction. Between a greed so far on its path to evil that there is no turning back and an institution for the lie that paved the path forward.

To enter this place is to touch history's ghost. I just hope the ghost does not fill my mouth and ears with silence.

24. Address

Go back to the address book, which was a 1942 leather daily planner
with my great-uncle's name and address embossed on the cover. My
great-aunt repurposed his planner. *The Employer's Group* appears
in gold script, stamped into the leather with a logo of an owl and a
crescent moon. And *The Service that Satisfies*. This was likely a
company gift that Albert, my great-uncle, never used. Bertha, my
great-aunt, carefully wrote the addresses of "Mom" in North Bergen,
NJ and someone by the name of "Titty Rabinowitz" in West Los
Angeles. How this little album with the crumbling spine and loose
pages came to my mother, I'm not sure. Or why it was saved. It
survived the first purge, when my grandfather's second wife donated
my grandfather's pilot uniform. And when M. pilfered my grandfather's
bomb ring the morning after the funeral — after some previously
unseen boxes came out of the crawl space. M.'s sisters wore my
grandfather's gold watches on their wrists to the wake. And wore
them home. They also picked some photos out of the war album my
grandmother had given to my mother, and that she left on the counter
to share while we grieved. Darkened squares appeared in the paper in
the where my grandfather's face was. They left the atomic bomb photo.
The atomic cloud hides in plain sight and obscures its own story. But
back to the crossed-out addresses. After all these years, was it purely
by accident that this small book became an accidental artifact? It
could be that someone, my grandfather, wanted to keep his sister's
handwriting after she died (why did Bertha's book go to him, and why
did he save it?). So small, the size of a deck of cards, the book with the
cracked leather cover could have easily wedged into an open edge of
a nearly full shoebox of trinkets. It could have hidden there and then

been crushed, trashed. Bertha wrote her Social Security number on the first page, under her name and her own crossed-out address. She also wrote that she owned a Bulova watch.

Thick ring with a bomb. Binding together the pilots who served under the same mission. When my grandfather died and things came out of his attic, my mother found the ring and gasped, and showed it to my brother who said, *I don't want that.* I thought he meant to hold it, to wear it on his finger. I watched all of this happening as though it were on TV. I didn't understand that people were grabbing possessions. My mother set it on the table with the album and it was gone in the morning.

These objects, these things, removed from context, held in the hand, in the mind, are infused with the past — or past-ness — and stripped from fact. From origin story. From owner. Instead of clues, they risk becoming relics.

If one of these relics hold meaning for you, they address you.
You are their audience.

I keep losing the notebook where I write down my ideas and research. Not on my desk. Not on my coffee table. Not in the bed, trapped in the sheets (I like to write in bed) or under a pillow. It feels like someone is hiding my progress from me. But that person is not a ghost but another version of myself.

✛ ✛ ✛

Recently, I saw Mary Magdalene's tooth. Mary Magdalene, disciple of Jesus, who saw him before anyone else after his resurrection. The tooth was at the Metropolitan Museum of Art, in a gilded container — a glass egg — and propped up on pedestal.

The tooth looked, well, toothy. The root attached. It had clung to a skull. It was real, as a tooth. It absorbed many prayers and petitions in Tuscany. Now this tooth appears with other objects taken from churches and temples and graves. You can walk through mazes of glass — cases full of cabinets. Chart your course through these objects that may or may not catch your reflection, your hand, your cheek, your hair. A carved face, the grief of having been taken from a sacred system, studied and placed here.

Mary Magdalene's tooth is a tooth.

✛ ✛ ✛

When I lived in one of my grad school apartments in Maryland, along the on-ramp to a highway, with my boyfriend and our roommate I'll call Carl, my mother called to tell me she lost my grandfather's wedding band. It had come to her after the funeral, I think, and she wore it with her other rings on her finger. But the gold circle slipped off — we think when she stopped by after the funeral. We couldn't figure out where the ring went.

One afternoon in late November, after I received a collections notice for an unpaid doctor's bill — I had passed out and needed a heart test, and part of it wasn't covered by insurance, or at least that's how I remember it, but this could have been any number of labs that the HMO wouldn't cover — I ransacked the common areas of our apartment when everyone was out. (It was rare for Carl not to be on the couch, writing his screenplay, but I was alone.) I searched the kitchen, looking for papers caught between cereal boxes on the counter. I looked in the living room underneath stacks of books. And then I saw a cardboard box that had become a catch-all for incoming mail and clutter. It was next to the TV. As I reached inside, my fingers brushed against something cold.

"There you are!" I said out loud, to the box and to the empty room combed with light.

With my pinky finger and thumb, I picked up the wedding band. The gold felt small and thin, though my grandfather's hands were much larger than mine.

My boyfriend (who would later become my spouse) and I had recently called off a wedding. We had gotten engaged after dating a short time. Things fell apart. That is a story for another time. But as I held the ring in my palm, the ring too loose for my violinist fingers, I felt like I had a visit from my grandfather. Maybe this was a blessing. Or a bit of tough love, which is how I read the memory now. (As in:

"Who screwed this up?") For a moment, holding the wedding band was painful. But then I laughed.

"You got me!" I said to the room. Ever mischievous, my grandfather had played a trick on me. He'd never been to my apartment. Yes, the ring slipped off my mother's hand. I was going to recycle the box of papers. The ring had been half-embedded in the overlapping cardboard flaps that formed the bottom of the box. Would I have noticed, decluttering in a hurry, crushing the box and tossing it in the recycling bins outside? So, the ring returned to my mother, and she would wear it around her neck on a gold chain.

✢ ✢ ✢

A ring, a tooth, an address book.

A thing takes on its own life.

It's by chance, really, that some objects enter and stay in your life. Without Bertha's address book, I wouldn't have information that my grandfather was in Alamogordo or Carlsbad, NM, or even his bomb wing number — nothing other than his story about being at White Sands and driving a jeep into the gypsum dunes.

✢ ✢ ✢

In 1941, my grandfather enlisted before his eighteenth birthday. He trained as a radio operator and mechanic — and would later work as an electrician in New Jersey after the War, until he retired. In 1944, my grandfather participated in "brief but intensive schooling" for pilots, bombardiers, and navigators. Here, they would acquire "technical knowledge and skill to become a leader and killer." The officer training manual says this: *for that is what we are to become — killers — equipped with the most murderous weapons for killing.* I always stop here. The sentence continues, *and our characters must meet the test of wielding our weapons with a mental reservation for forging an enduring peace.*

✢ ✢ ✢

I can't understand how my grandfather could be trained to think that he could become a killer — *equipped with the most murderous weapons for killing.*

✢ ✢ ✢

The gymnastics of the sentence that ends with peace is so swift and surprising, that I don't know what to say.

✢ ✢ ✢

Both atomic bombs, total, killed over 200,000 men, women, and children in Hiroshima and Nagasaki.

✢ ✢ ✢

Thomas Handy — Acting Chief of Staff while President Truman and Chief of Staff George Marshall were at the Potsdam Conference — authorized General Spaatz, Commanding General of the United States Strategic Army Air Forces to drop the "first special bomb as soon as weather will permit visual bombing after about 3 August 1945 on one of the targets: Hiroshima, Kokura, Niigata and Nagasaki."

In his memo on July 25, he also wrote, "Additional bombs will be delivered on the above targets as soon as made ready by the project staff."

The Atomic Heritage Foundation's description of the second atomic bomb blast also acknowledges multiple bombs: "The decision to use the second bomb was made on August 7, 1945, on Guam. Its use was calculated to indicate that the United States had an endless supply of the new weapon for use against Japan and that the United States would *continue to drop atomic bombs on Japan* until the country surrendered unconditionally."

About the possibility of a third bomb, Herbert Freis wrote in 1961 — in the book that I read and copied from by hand in the Main Branch of the New York Public Library on 42nd Street — that "because of an unforeseen increase in the rate of production of plutonium, all ingredients and components for the third bomb made for use against

Japan were all in hand in the United States by about August 10, and they could have been assembled in Tinian, and the bombs could have been dropped some days before August 20."

✤ ✤ ✤

The 316th bomb wing, which my grandfather was part of, was overseen by the commander that chose the site of the Trinity explosion in New Mexico. This bomb wing was then quickly moved to the Pacific — the earliest bomb group of this bomb wing, which I am almost certain my grandfather was part of because of the information in my great-aunt's address book (the bomb wing and bomb group numbers for my grandfather), arrived on Okinawa on August 8, the day before the Nagasaki bomb dropped. Another record I discovered states that they began arriving on the 6th of August, the day of the Hiroshima bombing.

✤ ✤ ✤

The US military dropped the second atomic bomb on Nagasaki, but this was the result of a quick change of plans. Major Charles Sweeney, pilot of *Bockscar*, was supposed to drop the bomb on the city of Kokura and tried three times to get visibility through smoke from wildfires and thick clouds.

My grandfather said he was there that day and part of the mission. Based on Bertha's address book, he was interviewed for the mission as he said he was at the Lincoln Air Force base in Nebraska. He "wasn't chosen" for the core fleet. But he wound up in New Mexico, connected with the Trinity atomic blast — the bomb which had the same core as the bomb dropped on Nagasaki.

"We flew so high the radar can't detect you," he'd said, and then clammed up, refusing to say more. My brother remembers my grandfather talking about being a decoy plane.

Japanese antiaircraft fire approached right during "the third bomb run," or the third time Sweeney tried to drop the bomb with the plutonium core on the city of Kokura. So, the plan changed — quickly — and the planes on the mission peeled away. As the Atomic Heritage Foundation reports, "Running low on fuel, the crew aboard *Bockscar* decided to head for the secondary target, Nagasaki."

✢ ✢ ✢

I was interested to read in the note about the possibility of a third bomb that Truman specifically commanded General Spaatz that "no third drop should be made unless specific authorization was sent to him."

What was or wasn't decided about the second bombing? The quick call that showered a city in nuclear fallout and instant death?

✢ ✢ ✢

I've read that the 316th bomb wing arrived "too late to participate in combat." And yet, this isn't true. They arrived before the war ended. They started arriving just before the atomic bombings. And yet they

were connected with the plutonium bomb exploded in the desert of
New Mexico, the bomb that then the very same day assigned them to
the Pacific Theater. Among all of the public flight rosters, I have yet
to find my grandfather's. I've studied the rhetoric of the Manhattan
project coverups, and often the denial of anything occurring
when something did in fact occur is the way the lie was crafted. The
redaction is a deletion and a negation.

✛ ✛ ✛

I cannot find information about where my grandfather's bomb wing
was stationed between June 1945 and August 5, 1945. July 16, in
New Mexico, the Trinity bomb exploded. August 6, the US Military
detonated the first atomic bomb in Japan.

✛ ✛ ✛

Here I am, holding a crumbling address book, that exists by chance,
or maybe this was my grandfather's way of saying he wanted to pass
along some hints at the truth. His bomb group, his addresses, and
proof he was at the same air base where interviews for the 508th
composite group (that he ended up not being part of) which officially
dropped both atomic bombs are in this small book.

What would it mean to see an atomic explosion and also know
that it would be dropped on citizens? What would it mean to fly
above the cities decimated by the force of the blast, by the fires, by
the fallout?

On the back of one of his photographs that he sent home to his parents, my grandfather wrote, "Send me home, I've seen enough." Standing near a torii gate in Okinawa, in another photograph, he looks haunted. Lost. Sometimes, he would pause and look off, faraway, even though his eyes could quickly glint with humor as he returned to himself. But I've never seen such a look of horror on his face.

25. Statue

"Statue!" I screamed.

Larger than our house, the shadow blotted out the sun in Des Plaines, Illinois near the river that would flood each year. Silver, swollen, the plane belly seemed weighted with more than luggage. And it lowered to the nearby runway at O'Hare, ready for landing, wheels down.

The wind and roar from the massive machine flattened the dry grass in the backyard separated by a chain-link fence from the neighbor.

Chelsea, my friend in the ranch house down the street, had been Hula Hooping with a bent green circle behind my ranch house with its brick and pale-yellow vinyl slats. We lived so close to O'Hare International Airport that I looked for my dad in the windows of the planes above us when he was away.

"Statue!" Chelsea screamed back, though I couldn't hear her.

Instead, I watched her lips move and her eyebrows scrunch together as the sun-bleached green and gold Hula Hoop swung around and around her skinny waist. On the way to kindergarten, she'd compare her slender legs to my thicker ones next to hers in the backseat of the car when her mother or my mother would drop us off at the square brick school building while "American Pie," already an "oldie," played on the radio. My Hula Hoop hadn't been at my waist. It had already dropped down so that I was standing inside the circle while the enormous airplane barreled over the roof.

As though in slow motion, while the sky momentarily darkened over us, the candy cane striped plastic circle dropped to Chelsea's frilly ankle socks and bounced off the top of her shoes. We both froze. The air smelled cooked, like hamburgers without the meat.

We could see people in the windows looking out, a blonde-haired woman in a green sweater who waved at us.

The planes would almost seem to land on the house, one after the other, especially in the late afternoon and early evening when we'd be home from school. You'd have to yell in the middle of a conversation inside the house, where my mother spoon-fed my baby sister peas from a jar.

"Airplane!" she called, the spoon with the green mush hovering in front of my baby sister's lips. We all stopped talking because we couldn't hear each other while the shadow darkened the kitchen window. Time stopped, then we became animated again after the shadow passed.

I remember my sister crying a lot at night. She must have been about one. We shared a room for a while until I ended up in a bunk bed in my brother's room. My father bought it second hand, the 2x4 boards spray painted a sticky black color that would splinter my palms. My father made sculptures then, and the bunk bed reminded me of one of his reclaimed wood works that he'd sometimes paint. At that time, I remember my mother singing to my sister, quietly. Curly light brown hair covered my mother's face, the baby swaddled on her lap while my brother and I ran circles around her. She was a little embarrassed we could hear her singing and switched from "Rock-a-Bye Baby" into a hum. In the evening, when she was putting the baby down, my brother and I caught lightning bugs in a Mason jar on the lawn, brought them into our room, and watched them pulse in the dark — me on the top bunk, closer to the sky. The little green lights far away, below on a shelf. I wondered how the city must look to a pilot. I closed my eyes, closer to the engines that rattled the window glass.

✝ ✝ ✝

What is a grandfather? I think of a grandfather clock. I think of an old book with some pages missing, the binding cracking. The "Greatest Generation" grandfathers were quiet about what they did. Bound to one another by the War. They crafted stories about it by disconnecting from the horrors they saw and made — the explosions, the death, the rubble. The "loose lips sink ships" mantra they murmured at dawn while tying their boots and cleaning their guns smoothed over the secret voice kept close between their ribs and heart muscle that told them the true version of their stories after rhetoric paved them over.

Grandfather makes me think of stillness, of contemplation, when I consider my mother's father. But this stillness is crafted from reflection, from a silence that comes from being made by a story that we tell ourselves about history. I think that is why I can't untie the word "historical" from the word "grandfather" in my mind when I think about the pilot grandfather I had.

Slightly younger, my other grandfather, my artist grandfather, who fought in the Korean War but didn't see battle, doesn't convey this stillness to the same extent. My artist grandfather was of a slightly different generation. He dipped his fingers in thick paint — drawing a grid, or a beetle, or a stylized portrait of the Queen of Hearts — and talked about his mother, a pianist, who raised him and his siblings alone. In 1928, in San Francisco, my artist grandfather's own father walked out the day he cried his first breath, never laying eyes on the baby that was my grandfather. And so maybe it comes from being born slightly later, just outside the 1901-1927 window of the "Greatest Generation" who fought in WWII and grew up during the Great Depression, or maybe it comes from the father wound and the well of love his musician mother gave him after moving back to upstate New York to raise him and his siblings near family, but my artist grandfather was not silent about the past. He didn't offer it in fragments, at least not to us. Connectivity and movement were all part of his personality. He and my grandmother, also an artist and art teacher (who planted zinnias and made Hopper-esque landscape paintings), shared a studio in their attic, climbing the drop-down ladder to paint in the creative space they made for themselves on weekends and evenings. Like his paintings, my artist grandfather drew comparisons between unlike things and incorporated fun into beauty. As an example, he took me to see the NYC ballet when they danced at the Saratoga Performing Arts Center in the summer. The dancers twirled on stage in tulle under the lights, performing a folk tale, and then we talked about the performance in depth while snacking on purple grapes — a treat — at intermission. Yes, we talked about the gestures and the story, but we also had a blast chatting about what we eavesdropped from the other audience members around us.

Both grandfathers loved me, I know. I'm fortunate I know this. And fortunate that I knew both of them. They were so different from one another that when I think about them now, the word grandfather means something slightly separate when I consider each of them. When I think about what I don't know, I consider how my pilot grandfather's parents didn't learn English and only spoke Czech, that my pilot grandfather was a first-generation American who enlisted to fight as young as he could. Not many of his family emigrated through Ellis Island, I learned. Most stayed in Bohemia. I have one of the few things from "the old country," a ceramic vase with flowers on it. Later, I learned the vase is a beer stein missing the lid with *One more round for the landlord!* written over its belly. My grandmother's mother had been in an orphanage on and off in Manhattan before getting married very young and eventually moving to New Jersey. My grandmother built tiny dollhouses out of wood, and I think about how carefully and seriously both she and her mother had taken the art of the home, with the inherited trauma of having it taken away in such recent memory. I remember my grandmother's workshop in her basement, how she loved to show us where she made dioramas out of wood and hand-crafted tiny furniture for the figures she placed there.

As I consider the atomic bomb cloud photograph caught in time over the city of Nagasaki after the crew changed course and bombed that city instead of Kokura, and as I consider the photographs of the New Mexico desert with soldiers all lined up to observe something momentous at the "White Sands" air base — what I am almost certain was the Trinity atomic bomb test — that my grandfather passed along to my mother (slippery photos all shuffled out of order in the album he said was "classified"), I think about what it means to hold a secret in your body your whole life.

My mother recently told me she remembered my grandfather saying the same thing, over and over, almost like he was snapping into attention, about the bomb. "It saved lives. It ended the war," was all he said, flatly. This is very different from the photograph of a bombed-out building he tucked into a letter to his parents — which his brother Charlie, who lived upstairs from them, received and translated for his parents. Scrawled in pencil on the back of one of the photos: *Send me home. I've seen enough.*

✛ ✛ ✛

And when I probe my memory of my pilot grandfather, the man not the story I'm telling about the man, the actual person, I ask what secret did his hands — spotted from the sun, thick with veins — carry from coaxing a plane into the sky? I can almost touch his hands in my mind. I remember them so clearly. And I remember them placed over his body after he died.

What role did he have, holding the flat metal circle with the magnetic needle in its dish of water that day a fleet of planes almost bombed a different city and wrought unconscionable destruction in another? And then almost ran out of gas and crash landed afterward on Okinawa?

He sat in the back seat with me after we picked him up from O'Hare.

"Whew, look at those planes," he'd say, staring at the passenger jets barreling over the highway. "They look like cigars. Boy, would I like one right now." And then he'd pause. "Sure is good to be in Chicago."

"We don't live in Chicago! We live in *Des Plaines!*" I corrected, which was one of our ongoing jokes. My grandmother didn't have endometrial cancer which became lung cancer then, so she must have sat up front with my mother, where they talked and laughed. Of course, my pilot grandfather loved looking at planes, talking about planes, and he was also fascinated by how close they'd pass over our ranch house situated so close to the tarmac. But I don't remember him playing "Statue" with us.

✝ ✝ ✝

As a child, I always thought that the name of the town Des Plaines, and its adjacent often-flooding river, referred to the airplanes from O'Hare blaring over our lawns, parks, schools, and train tracks. *Of course* the planes that smeared the sky in cotton-tufted, crisscrossing contrails were how the town got its name. Later, I assumed the name Des Plaines referred to the plains — the flatlands of the Midwest where if you look down a long straight road, the side edges will converge into a vanishing point, as though in a drawing. You can look forever ahead of you and see the path forward until it disappears. That is the illusion. Only now that I've acknowledged I do not know how Des Plaines ended up with its name and look it up do I realize that *des plaines* is "probably in allusion to the sugar maples (*plaines* in Miss. Valley Fr.) once there." The name came from French fur traders who settled the area and began the violence against the Council of the Three Fires, The Odawa, Ojibwe and Potawatomi Nations. Chicago comes from the Algonquin word meaning "onion." Where the air ripples with jet fuel and roaring engines, the land once rippled with ramps and wild onions.

A young sugar maple grew in front of our second house in Des Plaines, a little bit further from the airport and the river that flooded our first house.

Probably, writes the author of the entry for the etymology of Des Plaines, acknowledging any slips in the story. Like a statue with moss growing over the face and descriptive plaque.

✣ ✣ ✣

We moved to Des Plaines, but not one of the fancier suburbs, after a teenager was shot in the alley between the apartment building in Chicago that my parents had moved into as young artists without knowing about gang territories there. My brother was born when we lived in that apartment. My parents lived in two previous apartments when I was a toddler, if I'm gathering my facts correctly. But that building is my first memory of Chicago. In fact, one of my first memories is of young men sitting on the roof of the tiny garage behind the apartment building.

So while the swift, cloud-like shadows cast over our ranch house along O'Hare International Airport are part of one of my earliest memories, the edge of Humboldt Park and Logan Square in Chicago in the early '80s is my earliest.

After my parents moved us out of that apartment, the next owner replaced the wood door with a bullet-proof one. About ten years ago, I found that building, and the bullet-proof door is still there.

But I also remember a sunny kitchen with a white linoleum floor where I played with a shape sorter. The red triangle went into the triangle hole. I was praised. I was a toddler. My younger brother was a younger toddler. We pretended to talk — or at least, I did — and I knew that my speech wasn't really speech yet.

I remember narrow bedrooms, darkened in the daytime so the light looked maroon. I would not nap, and neither would my brother. My mom was trying to work on a weaving. She threw up her hands because my brother was crying. (As a mother now, I empathize that when you plan to use naptime, naptime doesn't materialize.) I remember a piece of burnt toast popping out of the 1940s toaster — with the fabric cord — my parents acquired at a flea market. The blackened toast flew through the air and onto the floor. We all laughed.

And then there was the black wrought-iron fence my dad put up around the two-flat casting blue shadows in the snow. A group of young men crouching on the roof of the squat garage out back while my mother nervously loaded me into the car. The stereo would soon be stolen, my mother's rings lifted from a drawer, a teenage boy my parents would talk to sometimes shot in the alley between our house and the next one. He was shot and left on the concrete or shot and left in a car there. The details are fuzzy.

I wouldn't know any of that, then. Only the men on the roof. After the boy bled to death, our parents moved us to the ranch house in Des Plaines.

I can see the boy in my mind. This can't be possible. But I remember him — his plaid shirt open at the neck.

So my early memories after these dream-like swatches are of growing up just past one of the major landing strips of O'Hare International Airport, in a Western suburb of Chicago with a diner where an electric train would bring you your pancakes on a track that looped the edges of the booths, where my father would take the L "downtown" in the morning and we'd wait out thunderstorms in the station wagon at the "kiss and ride." Every memory I have of that time is bound with the extreme noise of the jets and the layers of their needle-like flashes in the clouds and then lower, larger, as they circled and came home, almost on us, while we froze — mid-word. Contrails appeared as ghost writing and faded, first becoming dashes of script, then spots.

My brother and I would punch each other in the arm based on how many chocolate chips we counted in our Chips Ahoy cookies while we sat on stools at the counter in the kitchen, and then our laughter would be obliterated by an engine roar. We thought the red marks we gave each other were hilarious. We'd laugh after the noise, then we'd freeze again — *statue!* — when another plane barreled down over the roof, rattling the kitchen windows and stirring the curtains my mother sewed.

Being inside the ranch house when this happened was a thrill of its own because you couldn't see the silver machine's arrival. There wasn't a machine, and then there was. All of a sudden, the roar that would cancel all conversation, reset an interaction, become its own game.

"What if they land on the house?" I'd ask my mother.

"They won't," she'd answer, turning away to wash her hands. My little sister would crawl quickly into the living room after my mother put her down, and we'd pretend to crawl, too.

Now, if you're in an Uber or Lyft headed to O'Hare on I-90, there's a stretch where you can experience what this was like, where the planes seem to land on the highway and just appear — these huge shapes — loudly and out of nowhere above you. Even though I grew up in a house that would rattle as the planes came in, one after the next, the times I've seen planes almost land on the highway have shaken me, startled me. Everything wrong for a minute, then right again.

After my baby sister was born when I was five years old, I remember visits from both sets of grandparents in the ranch house that flooded one too many times before we moved to an old gray farmhouse, also in Des Plaines, a little farther from the river near a junkyard and a house where rows of corn had replaced the grassy front yard. I played violin in the window and tap danced in the garage. We lived in the Prairie Avenue house until we moved away on my twelfth birthday, to a tiny town in the North Country, so far upstate in New York it borders Canada. On the opposite bank of the St. Lawrence River houses fly Canadian flags. The day we left Des Plaines, the movers each signed a dollar bill and gave it to me before taking my bed.

Reluctantly, I climbed out. But later, I hid in a closet during the final walkthrough, tracing the dark corner with my finger.

✛ ✛ ✛

Leaving Des Plaines broke my heart. But when I returned to Chicago for five years in my late twenties and early thirties for grad school, starting out in an apartment a handful of blocks from where the teenager died in the alley when I was a toddler, I never went back to the place where we were statues. To Des Plaines. I don't know why. Some years, I didn't have a car. Then I did. But even then, I didn't exit the highway one Saturday, pausing in front of the maple that would now have a thick trunk. The maple I could see outside my window of the Prairie house. I didn't puzzle over the ranch homes close to the river, trying to remember which one was mine. In dreams sometimes, I walk past them, pausing at each door, stepping closer and closer to the river but never reaching the right home.

In a way, I wanted Des Plaines to be a place where part of me had stayed, arms on my hips, Bulls T-shirt on, squinting at the massive wings cutting the sun and freezing me in place.

✢ ✢ ✢

Sometimes it takes me a few minutes to realize I am crying. My cheeks wet, my eyes stinging. *What is on my face?* My fingertips brush my eyelashes. *Oh, I am crying.*

✢ ✢ ✢

My pilot grandfather would look out the backseat window while we drove home from O'Hare, pointing at the planes and saying, "You count to three and hope those landing wheels are down, *phsssh*." But he didn't say much more about his time in the USAF. And this is what I remember — what more would he say to a child? But he did not say much more to my mother, either.

But I can hear his New Jersey accent in my ears, how he pronounced "three" almost without the "th." Not tall, he was rugged, with a pointed chin that I inherited. He was trim and with mischievous blue eyes that held a bit of a twinkle. A navigator, he loved studying atlases.

"Do you live in Chicago?" he'd tease.

"No! I live in Des Plaines!" I'd correct.

He was loving, went by "Hank" among his friends and my grandmother, and he also had an edge. But he would play checkers with me, would do school projects with me when he visited and teach me about gears and friction.

For a long time, I confused *friction* with *fiction*. Even now I think about the tug on the truth. The heat that comes from the imagination.

A year before he died, when I tried to ask him about the bomb, he would get quiet and change the subject. Once he got angry. That was the time my brother, at that point a young adult, got him talking about that day, and my grandfather said something about flying very high, about being a decoy, and then he got angry at being questioned. The bomb dropped and didn't detonate right away. He flew so high. Something, something. Angry. He stood up — his impeccably creased pants still starched at the knee — and walked across the carpet criss-crossed with lines from my step-grandmother's neurotic vacuuming.

We pieced together that he had been talking about the Nagasaki bomb, and later, before his death, when he handed my mother a photo album filled with photos of "girls" smiling through dark lipstick that looks like shadows in black and white photographs. Young women with fluffy hair and long overcoats and stockings in Utah, Nebraska, etc. "She was nice," he'd say, his eyes filled with mischief.

Later, I saw the mushroom cloud photo. The Nagasaki cloud. "This is classified, but I guess it's OK for you to have this now," he had said of the book. I thought he was joking at the time, but when I saw the photograph, I began to understand that he wasn't.

It took me years to completely understand what "classified" might mean. Even now, I tangle with the word, which refuses access to certain information. Yes, so many historical documents can be found online. Yes, lots of the nuclear test films are declassified. Yes, you can search the FBI database. But classified means classified. The redactions like shadows in a text.

✢ ✢ ✢

Like puzzle pieces, each person working for the Manhattan Project connected with another person or small group, yet not knowing the whole picture. At least, not until the detonation. Somehow, this man who was my grandfather and took me out for ice cream also played a role in the horrific death and disease in a city in Japan, and in the wreckage that split the last century in half into a before and after.

A man who might look like a teenager to you, the age of a freshman in college or senior in high school. Testing into military units, being moved around the country, to New Mexico, and then, at just the moment in history when the US knew what its weapon could do and decided to drop it on another country anyway, to the Pacific Theatre.

This man flew over the silver sea, knowing what was to come. If I'm correct about his bomb wing, unlike most of the 509th composite group credited with dropping the bomb on Nagasaki — except for Navy Commander Frederick L. Ashworth, who had participated in the Trinity detonation in New Mexico — my grandfather had witnessed the atomic cloud before shipping out to the Pacific. If I'm right, his bomb wing knew what was at stake, had seen the odd geometry boiling into the sky.

What do you do to live with this? Swallow a story that sits uneasily in your throat? And then it lives there and becomes part of you, your voice. What do you say and not say? Mostly you do not say. Around this subject, a stillness accrues. As you age, as you sit back in your chair, the stillness becomes you. Nothing emerges from your mouth when questions fall onto your lap like hands.

✢ ✢ ✢

Grief freezes you in time, you can visit the old self contorted in pain or horror or sadness, walk around the form that you were, and try to talk to it — the old you who is also the you you are now.

My grandfather's oldest brother was *the violinist and darling child,* my mother says. He died on Memorial Day drag racing his cousin on a motorcycle. Faster, faster, into the darkness, then the wheel spun, and he flipped, smashing into the wall of the Holland Tunnel. After that, my great-grandparents never spoke to that side of the family again, not even at the funeral. Whenever I'm in a car idling in the fumes of traffic, in that primeval darkness in one of NYC's tunnels, I feel a deep unease. My throat catches. Even before I knew George's story, I felt a loss at some kind at that threshold between light and dark.

And then a car hit us one Friday, our third summer in New York, in the early evening, in the Battery Tunnel. First, I heard a smash — metal on metal, battle shields — and then the car behind us hit us. "No —" I said out loud, as my head slammed forward into my phone then snapped back into the seat. The concussion made me feel drunk, horribly, in the way that my body wasn't synced up with the present. I didn't know I was forgetting things at first, until I'd see the look on a friend's face, and I'd realize that I had been in a loop, retelling the story I had just told. "Bruised, your brain is bruised," the neurologist said. In the MRI machine, which felt like being on a bed in a morgue, I sobbed when the magnets started probing my brain. An alien being that did not love me was attacking my mind, trying to open it up and erase it. In the some of the images, my brain looks like water rippling in the breeze. I'd started to have a panic attack and begged to be let out.

I kept wishing that I could step back into the old me, just before the accident, on my birthday walking with my daughter and smiling. Before the accident, I'd frozen some of my birthday cake that we couldn't finish — funfetti and buttercream — and then later I'd cut a stiff slice, let it thaw on the counter, and eat it slowly, closing my eyes and imagining that I could erase the video of my life and be the person I was before my injury. Nothing would help the headaches, and when they came, I could not think. But I kept visiting the moment of the impact — how I said "No —," how my head hit so hard. Frozen there, in the moment of the impact.

And yet, and yet, in that descent into darkness under the water connecting one NYC borough to another, I say "thank you" to that statue of myself, to the still image in my mind of my body contorted, my mouth grimacing as my head smacks the stiff seat. My daughter was completely fine in her car seat and holding her stuffed cat, which functioned like an air bag. My spouse was completely fine. And I — I could have been much worse.

My great-uncle, after he downed some beer and agreed to the race, after he hopped on his bike and rode faster, faster, thinking he was winning — maybe some money — and cutting off cars in the tunnel under the city, was his last thought "No —" as he flew off his bike? Did he have time to think before the darkness took him?

My grandfather's parents grieved him silently. What did they say to one another in Czech in the darkness of their room? Grief became a presence. As soon as he could leave, my grandfather enlisted, lying about his age. Another brother never left, living in an apartment above his parents and translating my grandfather's letters home for them.

✢ ✢ ✢

After the teen died in the alley in Humboldt Park, Chicago, after my parents moved us to the ranch house near the river that flooded with the planes and their enormous shadows, they moved us to a two-story 1920s bungalow, also in Des Plaines. A little farther from the wheels pressing down, impatient to reach the ground. But still close to the massive international hub. That move, at age five, worried me because I thought that the ranch house's feelings would be hurt if we talked about the new house inside of it while we packed our boxes. I did love the new house eventually — with three friends a short walk away, and a playground, and an intriguing home on the way there where the owner kept a pet monkey you could see looking out the window sometimes. We lived near the railroad tracks and a dive bar and a junkyard.

Evenings, nights, these were much quieter — the planes passing overhead emitted a low rumble rather than a roar — and I would lie in bed listening to rain rustling the maple leaves out front through the window screen in summertime. I would line up my stuffed animals around me and talk to them. "Please bring Grandma back to life," I'd say.

I'd been told my grandmother died of lung cancer, and later my mother told me it spread from her uterus. Only recently did she tell me it started as endometrial cancer. "When she was gardening, a gush of blood — " my mother said.

After I asked the stuffed animals — a pink horse, a sun pillow, a doll with matted hair — to bring my grandmother to life, I'd have nightmares. Once or twice, I sleepwalked down the stairs. I've never done this since that time.

My pilot grandfather's wife made dollhouses by hand and bran muffins and wore a pageboy wig after she lost her hair to chemo. This is what I remember. And her voice saying my name. *Tyler.*

Grief is a tide pool. Sapphire patches, glittering rocks, white light too hard to look at — it all is changing when you can finally touch it. You stand at the edge of it all and think that what you have left is all there is, and then the blue becomes green, reveals more hazards — sharp shells, broken claws, sea stars, and shark teeth. But you cannot examine these artifacts for too long, or water will wash over you, and you will be pulled into the intertidal zone that swells and releases its force, that smashes the cliff, that never lets you stay long enough in one place to understand it fully.

The phone call came one hot August afternoon. We didn't have air conditioning in the Prairie Ave. house, and we would draw the long linen curtains over the living room windows to keep the air cool. So the house was cast in muted darkness, the air stale. A box fan whirred. I had been reading on the couch, one step behind in solving a mystery. I was wearing my new favorite T-shirt, the Chicago Bulls Three-Peat T-shirt with silver lettering. I'd watched the Bulls beat the Suns in the NBA finals. It was an epic game — legendary. Every kid in Chicago either watched it on TV or knew about it. I still have this shirt.

The phone rang, and my mother picked up the receiver, tugging the long, beige curly-cue phone cord halfway across the room to the table where we ate dinner and where she'd cut my bangs with silver sewing scissors.

My mother listened to something, then sobbed, stumbling to a kneel with one palm pressed flat on the wall. Then she turned away.

Instead of giving her this moment to grieve in private, which now I realized she would have wanted, I remember watching her before dropping my book and rushing to her to hug her knees. More than anything, I wished I could make everything better all the while feeling afraid that my mother was crying.

My grandmother's clothes appeared one day in a large box — tweed pants, a little too short for my mother's long legs. Did my grandfather bring them when he visited solo? I felt funny about the pants and shirts, like I was supposed to want to keep them but also that they clearly belonged to someone else. I don't know what my mother kept or what she gave away. Eventually, all of it would be gone.

✛ ✛ ✛

My grandfather visited that Thanksgiving without her. He'd lose himself in thought and could not talk about her. During this time, he grew a mustache, and his light blue eyes would sparkle with tears.

Only after my grandmother, who he met shortly after the War, died from cancer did my grandfather start offering tiny bits of information about his war experience. I wonder now if something about the life he kept with her made him feel like he had to look away from what he saw, what he did. That he wanted to protect her from it. He stayed in my brother's bedroom during that visit, and I remember standing there with my brother next to the fish tank when my grandfather handed us a copy of a book about the Enola Gay, the plane that dropped the atomic bomb on Hiroshima. We didn't understand why he was giving it to us.

"This is important. You should know about it." My brother's room smelled like glue from his model airplanes, one half-built on his desk. The little pots of black and olive-green paint were open from when my brother snuck in there while my grandfather stood next to the charcoal grill outside with my father in the cold November air. My brother stood next to me. My sister was downstairs with my mother. "I was there," my grandfather said. "I was interviewed to do this."

What was "this?" We didn't know or understand what he was referring to. In my memory, he holds one of my brother's models and shows us where he sat, what he did. His slightly upturned eyebrows raised, and he said, "I'm glad I wasn't picked." His light blue eyes looked far away, cloudy. Then he changed the subject and went downstairs.

This was shortly before he started dating the woman who would quickly become his second wife. She gave away his USAF uniform, much of his pilot memorabilia, and many other things — my grandmother's things.

My grandfather didn't enlist because had had visions of becoming a war hero. I say this because sometimes, someone says, "Maybe he lied" as though he wanted to get a pat on the back and have a part in the famous story. Some veterans did tell tall tales, I know. But if this were the case, why wouldn't he have said more, created a full story that he could brag about? Why didn't he talk about it when my mother and her siblings were young, or when I was young? No, what he saw and what he did were secrets for a reason. Something he lived with and carried with him, like text redacted from a typewritten memo. Something swallowed into history's throat.

Military service was his ticket out of his life as it was — to travel, to wear new clothes, to eat plates and plates of meat and drink glass after glass of milk, as he wrote about in one of his letters home. He couldn't have known what he would see, what he would do.

As a kid, he wore his older sister's shoes to school. What did the leather tongues feel like against the bones of his feet? How did his heels slip out of them, a half-size too big? What shape did the toe scuffs look like, and did his older sister drag her toes behind her when she walked so that they flattened a bit? Did the other boys simply accept that he was wearing girl shoes? I doubt it. I imagine them pummeling snowballs at his head, calling him names as he walked to school.

But he couldn't have been the only younger brother wearing his sister's shoes to school those early autumn New Jersey mornings, while the jagged Manhattan skyline came and went in the fog shrouding the river.

Either way, I'll never know.

The shoes he wore belonged to the sister who would later write down all of his service records and addresses in the leather-bound calendar she repurposed into an address book. She couldn't let him go, and she kept this book until her deathbed, then gave it to him.

✛ ✛ ✛

All of these stories occupy a box in my mind like the cardboard banker boxes I stuffed with thank-you notes and letters from friends I haven't seen in years, Christmas and Hanukkah cards along with photos of baby nieces who are now teenagers hiding behind their hair in Zoom calls. And there is the birth announcement of my sister's son in a Santa hat. And there's the letter she wrote in purple ink and mailed to the house I rented when I moved to Las Vegas, New Mexico, before moving to Santa Fe. Disorganized, this mess is now stacked into a small fort along the wall in the new-ish, sunny apartment in Brooklyn. I go through it bit by bit.

This apartment doesn't have room for me to keep these archives I have carried with me. When we take the air conditioners out of the windows, those machines now must sit at the bottom of the closet, pushing the boxes out. Sometimes, I cannot focus while I am sorting the papers, so they become piles that I then tidy later, back into the box. Or I'll recycle some of the letters but can't let go of others. *What if my great-aunt's calendar, her address book were thrown away?* I wonder. The magic of an archive is what has been unexpectedly kept. I've moved so many times since college and grad school that in the last-minute packing frenzy, I've often swept papers off my desk and into these boxes, moving them, and then half-ignoring them until the next move or going through some of them but never completely finishing sorting and recycling the contents.

But part of the work of memory is uncovering the forgotten — not these little scraps of paper or old photos. Throwing out an old photograph does not make the person in it disappear. As I write from my little desk by the window in our bedroom in NYC where a garbage truck just roared by, I allow myself the light and space to say goodbye. To claim what writing can actually do — fully and completely. To be a way to converse with the past, to reckon with the statue you've made of your former self, to accept that what you remember is enough because that memory is now the story. Who you are now is part of it and the shape you make with it.

Between playing statue, we wiped black powder off the vinyl slats of the lawn chairs rusting at the hinges in the back yard. We breathed benzene, xylene, toluene, and formaldehyde. When I was seven, I came down with double pneumonia, and my lungs sounded like they spoke — whispered, choked, spat, scolded. They knew what I did not know, this voice outside of my throat, deep in my chest, close to my heart. I drank vile purple medicine from plastic cups. I stayed home from school so long that when I returned, the kids whispered that I had cancer and wouldn't talk to me in the hall for a while. Eventually, it was as though I had never been gone and eased back into the sticky-fingered PBJ-play of recess. As I climbed up the metal barred geodesic dome so many hands had grabbed that the slippery traffic yellow coating wore into a gritty silver, I watched my shadow move with me. Then I watched an airplane shadow puncture the shadow me.

Sometimes my lungs become this voice again, a sound like bubbling water when I walk along the Brooklyn Queens Expressway. Worse when we lived two blocks from the major artery between the boroughs and in summer when the pollution alert on my phone pops up on the screen. Now slightly father away, I cross the ocean rush of traffic, pass the little park with multicolored animals chained to the fence above the rush of engines and sirens from the BQE, and push a stroller to the playground with the sprinklers across the major highway.

Shallower and shallower the balloons of my lungs become on these walks, yet I love the smell of the traffic. Lightheaded, déjà vu floods through me — that comforting touch of the past — and the cooked scent of PM2.5 pollutants makes me feel like I am home. My lungs will later purr and wheeze, as though speaking through another dimension. I cannot discern what they are telling me, but I suck on the pipe of my inhaler and remember the little backyard in Des Plaines with the tree I'd talk to.

Mothering is not a verb that I can fully understand. My daughter loves me, pushes me away. Shuts her door on my foot. Demands I return. Powders my face with air kisses. Kicks me in the eye. Surfacing sometimes is a primaeval fury at being stuck in the tunnel of my body for so long.

My memory of the birth pain fades, but its artifact remains. My child.

When my infant daughter scrambled onto my chest, refusing to scream after clinging to the inside, to the tunnel between death and life, I placed my right hand on her wet back — not wet with me, but wet with the sea, with starlight, with a field of buttercups — and my left hand on the burnt umber cord. The umbilical cord felt like synthetic rope tied to a boat and slick with salt. When I touched it, I felt like nerve endings should be there on the rope. That the rope should allow me to feel my own fingers pressing on it. But plastic-like on my skin, the cord had already become not-me, like the purse of my placenta that the doctor collected in Tupperware and then disposed of.

✢ ✢ ✢

When my grandmother died, I was a young daughter who did not understand a link in the matrilineal rope, submerged now in the waters of the underworld with all the other strands.

Soon after, my pilot grandfather married his second wife and announced that he would be buried with my step-grandmother in a military cemetery in Virginia and not in the sloping hillside cemetery in Vermont where my grandmother's bones waited for him in a double plot. The children grieved this, my aunts and uncle arguing with him in the new home he shared with my step-grandmother.

Shortly before our visit, she had feverishly vacuumed, leaving the plush blue carpet crisscrossed. "I'm so tired," she'd said, and went to the bedroom.

My cousins and I made footprints that looked like dance steps on the carpet. While the adults argued, their voices rising, one of my cousins took all of our step-grandmother's decorative stuffed bears off the fireplace mantle and hid them under the couch and in a closet.

After that, our visits were much shorter.

✛ ✛ ✛

During a short visit soon before my grandfather's fatal heart attack, while my step-grandmother bustled in the kitchen over egg salad and saltines, I sat with my mother on the couch. My grandfather shuffled into the room in his slippers, holding out a black photo album. The edges crumbled, and the spine seemed to crack in his hands. Here it is, the album. This memory again.

"Here," he said. "Have this." And he gave it to my mother, who opened it over her lap.

Young woman after young woman appeared, lipstick-ed, smiling. I felt embarrassed seeing all of these young women, younger than me, linking arms with him.

"Oh, she was pretty. And whew, she was fun," he said, whistling. *Cringe. I don't want to hear this.*

Utah, Nebraska, Chicago. Later, looking through these photos after he died, I couldn't quite place where each had been taken. Bomber planes. Canvas tents. An unmarked navy cruise ship. Some aerial shots blurred. A photo of a plane landing. And there was my grandfather grinning in a cockpit. And there he was sitting with a young man who looked young and lost. The man seemed to follow him — there they were eating in the mess hall, there they were leaving a tent.

"This is classified. But I suppose you can have it now. It's been such a long time," he said. *OK, Grandpa*, I thought. *Right.*

My mother tried to give the album back, but my grandfather held up his broad hands. He didn't touch the album again.

Later, when I paged through the album, I gasped.

There was a photo of an atomic cloud towering in the sky.

And a photo of Hirohito surrendering on the *USS Missouri*.

And later than that, when I tried to ask him about it, he said he was there. And then, the narrative I grew up hearing: "the bomb let the US end the war."

And then, much later, I noticed the jeep, the photos of the desert, and I pieced the address book locations and bomb wing number with the pictures.

I've jigsawed the past together with fragmented memories, with scenes that I understood one way as a child and now I consider another way as an adult, with limited information.

Once, before we moved away from Chicago, before he married my step-grandmother, when he wandered through our home as though he had forgotten what he was looking for those months after my grandmother died, we stood in the yard. He looked at the sky.

"Why didn't you fly one of those planes? Work as a pilot after?" I'd asked as we watched one cast a slim shadow over us.

"They didn't want us — we didn't play it safe," he'd said.

But this wasn't true, as later I learned of WWII pilots working for US airlines, crisscrossing the country over and over, carrying people not bombs.

Only later would I glimpse the cracks in his story.

Why wouldn't he continue to fly? What would he see and do?

One time, shortly before he died, my grandfather turned to me out of the blue and said, "You should write true fiction." *Nonfiction*.

What do you say when the absolute truth is inaccessible, hidden? You study the shadows and ask what they tell you.

✢ ✢ ✢

My grandfather split up photos of Okinawa and New Mexico in his album, mixing them up. He didn't create a chronological narrative. The comingled, curled photographs of young pilots in military garb grinning in rows underneath the massive propellers of a B-29 or posing in front of a clapboard shack or pointing up at the pinup girls distorted over the nose of these death machines dissolves the what, when, and where of what happened. A stretch of desert where men in uniforms line up and face the distant mountains. Palm trees. The sea. My grandfather in a jeep. The effect of these juxtapositions, where one place bumps up next to another, one moment in time placed with another, is past-ness, a wash of historical imagery in photo after photo. The bombed-out cities. Pockmarked buildings, ruins, jagged and gray. And then — the bomb. With planes in my grandfather's bomb wing fanning around it.

Later after my mother picked all the yellowed, fading photos out of the paper photo corners and put them in a plastic basket for me to look through — and only then, when they were freed from the anti-narrative arrangement, when I sorted them into piles based on the kinds of uniforms, land formations, trees, and equipment — I started to understand. I recognized the New Mexico photos and put them in a pile. I did this with the others. And as I did, I repeated the words, *This is classified,* in my mind, and asked, *But what, what — other than the photo I would expect?* Why did he shuffle the rest of the photos, talk about the album as a whole? And then I saw it: the jeep, again. I remembered the story my grandfather told me about getting lost in the White Sands dunes in his jeep. And the numbers on the jeep, *316 BW,* confirmed the note in his sister's record. One photo was taken before sunrise. One photo after. Before and after. Similar poses. The *316 bomb wing,* of which Roscoe C. Wilson was the Chief of Staff. He had chosen the site of the Trinity bomb blast in New Mexico.

✣ ✣ ✣

When I filled out the service request form at the National Personnel Records Center housed in the National Archives, I didn't quite know what to write. Laughably to me now, I thought I'd receive a packet of helpful information in the mail within a few weeks. In any case, during this naïve phase of my research, I typed into the online form that I was seeking any information about where my grandfather was stationed during the Second World War, particularly in 1944 — 45. Once I submitted the form, providing my mailing address where records could be sent, a text box popped up on my screen:

Success!!!

Service request has been completed successfully.

And yet, the NPRC also sent me this statement:

You selected Other as relationship to Veteran, therefore, proper authorization may be required. Without the Authorization Signature of the veteran, next-of-kin of deceased veteran, veteran's legal guardian, authorized government agent, or other authorized representative, only limited information can be released unless the request is archival. No signature is required if the request is for archival records.

While I waited for even "limited information" to arrive, I asked my mother to fill out the form as next of kin. She said she would and closed her laptop.

The sweet smell of pollution — not dust, not perfume, not sulfur, but a scent like a color, pink and blue, like a dirty cloud. This is what I associate with home. In my apartment in Brooklyn that lets in a square of Southern light, my spider plant grows glossy on the deep windowsill next to the oven along with the tall pink flower that blooms and sheds its petals every few months. My daughter grew this flower from seed at the preschool she attended this year in a mask and presented it to me in an organic fibered pot on Mother's Day. Her nose rubbed red from her cloth mask, she looked at me with bright eyes and tried to hand the plant to me but ended up hugging the leaves closer to her ribs and chest. Her growth. Her creation. She couldn't quite part with it. So we share it with the sun in the kitchen. Each morning, as I let the tap run for two minutes to run any lead out of the water before making coffee, I open the window, water the plants, take a deep breath. Garbage trucks churn by. Sometimes, clean and leafy, the air hits my nose. Sometimes, smoggy, thin. This thin air hits my brain like a puff from the inhaler I need on days like this. Lightheaded. Later, I might check my phone and see that there is an air quality alert. And today, this combines with a toxic cloud of smoke that has arrived from the wildfires burning in the Southwest.

But before I know anything about this, I find myself smiling, lightheaded, and feeling a sense of déjà vu. Jet fuel. O'Hare traffic. The smell of something almost being grilled — an oven smoking burgers, or charring them, yet sweet, like being hugged, I really can't quite explain this scent. It reminds me of standing in the backyard of our ranch house before it flooded and stretching out my arms while a massive airplane barreled down on the yard and over the house.

So I walk through the ash and oak trees on the day that the forest fire smoke cloud swallows the city in sunset. Before the wheeze fully forms into little bubbles, like sticky tapioca pearls that clump into phlegm, the tickle feels like someone writing in pencil inside the lining of my lungs. The sound comes from somewhere else. Lung hum. Lung song. And I forget words, forget what I had been saying.

I pause, feeling the thick hot air, listening to the blurring sounds under the bridge. Frozen in time, for a moment. My muscles caught, mid-motion.

And so, against my better judgment, I say yes, I will visit the place where time stopped. Where the world began its end. Where poison unleashed its fire over the nation. Where the evil plan, hatched, became tangible. I will go to this meadow on a currently active military weapons test site. I will go in early autumn. I will stand at ground zero of the story. In standing there in stillness, I will become a part of that place. *Statue.* The shape of my body, the tilt of my head, my arms, my legs — all of this will stay in time, become part of the history. Even if I don't know what to make of it. Even if none of us can. My shadow will be my body's absence, in that moment of stillness. Like my grandfather's shadow also casting its shape over the soil, there, before his lips were sealed. My being there will be a representation of presence, of understanding. I will look when all I want to do is back away.

IV.

26. Boot

Last night, I checked into this hotel at three a.m. after checking out of the other hotel in Albuquerque where a spry cockroach jumped — flying, really — from underneath the pillow to the bedside table during my routine bed bug check. I'd talked my way out of my Hotwire booking standing in the bathroom while I also noticed a little smear of brown blood on the white tile floor.

The cockroach scurried behind the bedside table, after I grabbed my luggage. I strode to the glass door, past the drunk man a good ten years younger than me who looked me up and down with bleary eyes and said, "Helllllloooo" before stumbling into the dark hallway. Got into an Uber driven by a college student who was picking up riders the night before the first balloon rise — he wanted to bike along I-25 to the Balloon Fiesta the next morning and feel the cool, predawn wind in his hair and wake up eating a breakfast burrito underneath the enormous, newly risen orbs. Checked into the other hotel, having miraculously found a room during the city's busiest weekend of the year, almost 800,000 spectators, and cringed as my credit card swiped the machine at the check-in counter. Ghostly hands scooping the funds out of my account. Took a free Red Delicious apple waxed and polished in a basket at the reception desk. Slept until a stripe of sunlight pried through the blinds. Tomorrow morning, I'd wake in the dark and drive to the Trinity Atomic Test Site.

And now, as I unzip my suitcase, I realize my Tom's hiking boots wrapped in the plastic bag I saved from my favorite Thai restaurant in

Brooklyn — I can almost smell my favorite green curry, eggplant, and soft chicken soaked in coconut milk — take up half of my luggage.

What do you do with your shoes after you step onto the dirt of a nuclear test site?

Thick rubber soles with a tread that will press a footprint in the dust, like an astronaut, behind you.

Fluffy faux fur at the ankles, the heavy heels brought me to the petroglyphs and up and between the red-stoned passageways of Kasha-Katuwe Tent Rocks and to work in a skirt and leggings when I lived in New Mexico.

Will I bunch up the laces with the wax tips — a detail I always liked about shoelaces, even from the first bunny-ears bow I tied — and stack the boots, Tetris-like, back into the same white bag *(reuse, recycle)*? Wedge both boots under my pilling pajama pants and *Shine On* T-shirt I bought on clearance for three dollars when NYC was on lockdown? Then check the suitcase at the Albuquerque Sunport, carrying minorly radioactive particles into the open belly of the plane and back, like magic beans from a fairy tale, like breath from a god, the godhead blast, the first of this poison, back into my life?

Into yours?

What if I told you that after I pulled into the hotel parking lot, after walking in the radioactive dirt, I opened the driver's side door, swung my legs out of the car, propped up my right foot & looked at my heel & found, embedded in the boot tread, a blackish green chunk of Trinitite? That I walked off the site with this shard of melted glass from the atomic bomb blast in my boot?

What if I told you the evidence that we've engineered an end of the earth pressed down on the floor of the rental car while my toe bed pushed the touchy accelerator down, down, faster, faster, flying me away from the circle in the desert that smells sweet with meadow grass and attracts white butterflies in the purple milkweed?

27. Afterimage (X)

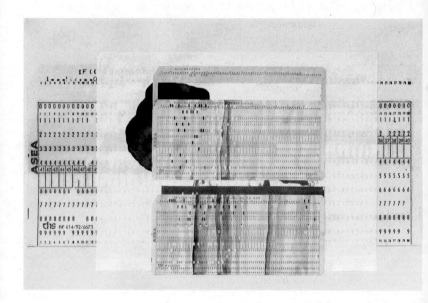

I bled earlier than some. My period came once while I stayed with a cousin. We shared the bed. I remember smooth pink sheets. Fluffy white comforter. I don't remember my dreams, or if I dreamt. She taught me how to make flowers out of beads, and I'd loop daisies in bracelets while I sat cross-legged on the carpet. One of those mornings, I woke up wet. I sat up and saw a red dot underneath me. Rosebud stains where I slept. Now I remember. I sat on the carpet stringing yellow and blue beads on fish line because she refused to let me sit on the bed after. The next year, I wore a liner *just in case*, even though it wasn't my time. I turned back the comforter. Polka dots of blood. Specks and dabs all over the sheets. Not fresh. *Oh, those are my friend J's,* she said when I asked.

28. Method

The backs of the photos I had examined at the Photo Archives in Santa Fe had been scrawled in graphite pencil with the f-stop number of the camera lens used to take the picture. Someone had also labeled them with the number of seconds after the blast that the image recorded. At one point I had written this information down, but I lost it — and myself in the popcorn-ball clouds.

In the cloud brains.

29. Cards and Clouds

When I made the *Afterimage* visual essays, I never imagined that the world would be bracing itself for the possibility of a nuclear strike. That shortly after Russia invaded Ukraine, there would be a run on potassium iodide pills.

Wash your hair with shampoo but not conditioner, as the chemicals will bind radioactive material to your hair.

It is important not to forget that not long ago at all, during the Trump presidency, Guam residents were told to "take cover" and not to look at a fireball. Guam, caught in the crosshairs of the nuclear missile crisis between the US and North Korea, is just about the distance from the Marshall Islands as New York and California.

According to the Atomic Heritage Foundation, in a little over ten years, "between 1946 and 1958, the US detonated 67 nuclear devices in the Marshall Islands," poisoning residents and literally wiping the island of Elugelab off the face of the earth. After one test where US scientists miscalculated the force of the Castle Bravo bomb, fallout affected islands that had not been evacuated. Jeton Anjain, a senator of the Marshall Islands Parliament who died of cancer in the 1990s, reported that "[a]pproximately five hours after detonation, it began to rain radioactive fallout at Rongelap. Within hours, the atoll was covered with a fine, white, powdered-like substance. No one knew it was radioactive fallout. (...) The children played in the snow. They ate it."

✢ ✢ ✢

Imagine hearing your cell phone emergency alert go off, picking it up, and seeing this in bold across your screen?

BALLISTIC MISSILE THREAT INBOUND TO HAWAII.
SEEK IMMEDIATE SHELTER. THIS IS NOT A DRILL.

If you lived in Hawaii in 2018, those words would have flashed
across your phone. You'd have a moment to wonder if you had
time to text *I love you* to your dear ones before taking cover as best
as you could.

The alert was false, as you might remember. An employee pushed
the wrong button, issuing the alert across the Hawaiian Islands.

What exactly caused such a gross miscommunication? What
crack in the system let such a terrifying alert break open the story we
tell ourselves that we are safe? And what does it mean that over and
over, we're at the precipice of nuclear disaster?

During my research for the poems in *Hawk Parable*, as I viewed
one declassified nuclear test film after another, I felt sick with horror.
Horror each time an atomic cloud blossomed above the glassy Pacific
waves of the Marshall Islands, throwing them into chaos. Horror
each time an atomic bomb cloud glowed into a fireball above the pink
desert of the Nevada Test Site where military personnel would often
stand, back to the camera, and watch.

I'd scrawl transcripts of these test films into the sketchbooks
where I had been drafting poems, pausing the video so I could copy
the voice word-for-word in my own looped handwriting. I'd request
scientific reports of bird migrations through the Nevada Test Site
from Interlibrary Loan and read them cover-to-cover, copying out

information about bird movement through the regions where fire would still be burning in the brush after a detonation.

I was like a magpie foraging for data, collecting fragments that were becoming too cumbersome for the nest I was building. The more I read, the more I needed to know. And the more I learned, the more I realized how much I *didn't* know.

As for the computer punch cards that became part of the collages, some of which had been punctured with holes and some of which had remained unrecorded? The paper rectangles seemed somehow emblematic of my encounters with information tied to the Manhattan Project and all of its mysteries.

Empty holes.

A programmer had once marked some of the cards with data important to the individuals who worked at the Los Alamos labs (the hours they worked and how much they would be paid). And now I could hold the cards up to the light and look through the perforations.

Through the gaps, I could see the tree outside my window unfurling with new leaves. My fingers touched the holes in the cards, and I thought about what little information I could access. The spots of light appearing in the redactions.

30. Trinity

Trinity Blast Crater Open House
Stallion Range Center Gage
5 miles S of US Highway 380
12 m. East of San Antonio, NM
Trinity Site is 17 miles from Gate
8 AM — 2 PM, closes at 3 PM
Exit 139, 380 East
Right exit 525, Stallion Camp Site
"Stallion Range Center Access"
1 ½ hours

Rise at 5 AM
Leave at 6:30 AM

Cash. Sunscreen. Hat. Water. Snacks.

I jotted down these directions in my notebook in case I couldn't get
cell service close to the nuclear test site. And so I would be organized
and feel prepared. Inside, I was anything but calm. My stomach
flipped as I looked at my notes. Nothing can prepare you for the place
that is nowhere and yet here — the place that grows with creosote
and wildflowers where we unleashed a fire that ripped open the sky.
You can feel the presence of something powerful there and you can
feel nothing. An energy that has the structure of something sacred
yet is the opposite. Like raspberries that smell sweet and black and

rotten. The berry and the death. Not a church of earth, this place. An enchantment, a spell — where everything is wrong.

I would go to the forbidden soil. Guarded with weapons, gates, checkpoints, and with a wall of wind that catches and swirls between the San Andres and Oscura Mountains.

When I would leave that place, that haunted circle inside a fence where rattlesnakes flick the beads of their keratin tails, I wanted to forget I was ever there.

✢ ✢ ✢

A fog skirt ruffled at the base of the San Andres mountains that October morning. Just at sunrise, the wheel of light bore into me sideways, like a searchlight. The mountains shimmered pink and purple. Once the sun rises in the desert, everything brightens immediately. The low sun became a brilliant orb illuminating the hood of the car, my hands on the wheel, and the roofs of the cars in the caravan ahead of me.

I took a photo with my phone, and the white spot of the sun on the screen looked as low in the sky as my grandfather's photographs of what I think are from the White Sands Proving Ground, established July 9, 1945 (now the White Sands Missile Range). He's lined up in a row with many other rows of army men in the desert all facing away from the camera, toward something. He's the only one — other than the high-ranking officials I still can't place who pose in front of the men and smile at the photographer — who looks at the camera. Their faces are grainy, blurred when enlarged. My grandfather's expression, which I looked at through a magnifying glass, is difficult to read. My grandfather marked himself in pen with a line on the photograph. That is how I initially found him in the crowd. But once I spotted him, his face — though gestural — was unmistakable. I'd know his sharp face anywhere. As he glances at the photographer, he looks dumbfounded and wise.

He and the shadowy generals look at the camera lens. No one else of his rank does. The young man is a witness that refuses to be fully part of the story of being a witness. He is eyeing the authority behind the decision, staring down the machine that takes account of that day. And then never speaking a word of it to anyone.

If he's witnessed the explosion, this photo was taken shortly after, I think, since the bomb detonated into a dark sky. I too woke before sunrise in New Mexico, the sky smeared with purple, at five a.m. I saw the crescent moon above the Starbucks and Burger King across the street from the hotel in Albuquerque.

In his photo album, my grandfather shuffled his pictures so the places, chronology, subjects, and characters intermingle. It was only when I tried to connect photos to places he was stationed after I studied the light, the plants, the dirt, and the uniforms that I realized the jeep he posed in front of a few times, in sunlight and in darkness, with his nickname and bomb wing number painted on the door, was what he drove around White Sands when he was stationed in Alamogordo, according to the address book his sister kept of his whereabouts. And then, it was only when I tried to find out more information about his bomb wing and came up with conflicting reports — statements about what they did not do — that I discovered online one page of a congressional hearing from the height of the Cold War linking his bomb wing with the Trinity Test Site. It was only then that I saw these photo in a new way: the jeep photo and the photo where my grandfather turns and peers right at the lens of the camera in what looks like the New Mexico desert. The military men in rows. All spectators of something. My grandfather looking back, regarding the story of the event as it was being recorded. Questioning it? Maybe.

Can I prove any of this definitively? No.

Just past San Antonio, past the Owl Bar, across the Rio Grande, is where you get to the Stallion Gate north of the White Sands Missile Range. This San Antonio, not the site of Texas's battle with Mexico, is a town where a hundred people live at the Northwest corner of a military weapons test site. Snow geese and sandhill cranes arrive in the winter — thousands of wings in the air. A friend told me how she laid down in the dirt there during the migrating season, spread out her arms, and watched the thunderous rush of feathers cascade over her body. As I had passed through the town of San Antonio, New Mexico I didn't see any birds. Instead, shrubs, jumping cholla, a yellow-green grass, and a handful of buildings dotted the landscape as the sun began combing the road in front of me and the land on either side of me in wands of light.

The White Sands Missile Range is the size of Rhode Island. It occupies a grayed-out box in the center of the state on Google Maps. Even in September, when I was reluctantly planning to go to the Trinity "open house" the first weekend in October, I thought I would be driving to Alamogordo, a military town now the site of the Holloman Air Force Base. A place I had been before. But as I read and reread the protocol for the visit, I realized that the atomic blast area is actually much closer to Albuquerque than I thought. And that the northern entrance, the Stallion Gate, is an encouraged entry point for travelers coming to the twice-a-year visits to the blast crater that the White Sands Missile Range authorizes for civilians. I would access the site, which sits close to the north edge of the Missile Range, from Albuquerque — a fairly short drive away.

Even though I'm trying to describe what it felt like to be there — to stand at the point on the surface of the earth where humans realized we could destroy the world — I'm struggling. *It's real, it's real,* we all thought as we entered the fence. You can look at hundreds of photographs, read reports about the detonation, but standing in an actual field stretching out emptily all around you — that is when you feel it. The unearthly power. The immense nothingness that isn't nothing at all. Mesmerizing, enchanting — when you enter the fence you feel like yourself and like you've stepped out of yourself. You begin walking, looking at the soil, at the sparkling green stones. You might think you'll whisper a prayer. Ask for forgiveness. *I'm sorry, I'm sorry. Please save us from ourselves,* you might begin. But you'll fill with something else. You'll forget what time it is, how long you've been standing at ground zero of the first nuclear blast. Though the landscape looks normal, the subatomic particles in the ground and in the sky carry the memory of the violence and its indescribable geometric light. The energy to create and destroy. Like a godly presence, this power — but infinitely selfish.

The reason that the death smell is so repulsive is that it carries the smell of life within it. I learned this when my upstairs neighbor died a month after I stepped onto radioactive soil, died in his apartment in New York City. After that, flies came for his corpse and appeared in the drain of my kitchen sink. Then the police arrived, then the detectives, then the morgue, which wrapped his body in plastic and threw it down the stairs. And then his death smell lingered, the super opened the hall windows, and we lived with Death until the air cleansed it, eventually, months later carrying the anger and darkness away into the great nothing that will swallow us all.

The atomic test crater carries life within its power structure, but the energy is the exact opposite. Evil, I later thought, can masquerade as goodness.

I don't want you to feel like you were there. I don't even think that I could fully communicate what being there is like. To do so, I'd need to harness the power that steals your breath. Its lips to your lips. Its hands to your throat. And now that I was there, I wish that I had never been there.

No longer a crater, the nuclear test site looks now like only a place. New Mexico extends all around it. And has blended within it. I hate that you can bring a Geiger counter and it will start beeping faster, faster. That there are "Do Not Enter" and "Radioactive" signs bleached by the sun chained to the twisted fence. How the wind fingered the gaps in the fence so it looks like bullet holes ripped through the metal in places. *From the explosion?* someone asked. *No, the wind* — the wind is the answer. Those holes are only where nature has pulled and won the warning. Soon, there will be no warning, only an enchantment. I hate how the wildflowers, purple and yellow, glitter in the morning dew before the desert borrows the moisture back. Hate that I loved these flowers and felt closer to a God I doubt and love before I realized this is the place that we tried to take life away from God. How the clouds hang in scarves below the mountains and burn off. How I can see the gypsum sand in the distance and think it's snow. That I said all this and am saying it again.

The beauty of the meadow grass in the light looked like a backlit photograph. The sun warmed my cheeks and I briefly felt peace. Fat ants slipped in and out of holes in the earth.

Maybe I will become ill one day and blame this place. But locating the blame and pinning it to a single decision and action will be impossible. All we've touched can contribute to our death.

As I write this, Putin has invaded the largest nuclear reactor in Europe. I watched on TV a fire burning there with reports that fire fighters couldn't get inside.

To enter the White Sands Missile Range from the north, you turn onto a long, narrow road through creosote and meadow grass, surprisingly green and sweet smelling. Twice a year, the public lines up here. Otherwise, the road stretches out, empty.

I thought I'd be early, but my rental car slowed and idled behind a long line of vehicles stretched so far ahead of me I couldn't see the beginning. People from the SUV in front of me — a family, I'd learn — got out, linked arms, and took a photo in the road in front of the fog-draped mountains. I got out of my car, too, and stood in the road, leaving the engine running, the door open. Everyone in the car ahead of me got back in except for one person with cropped hair and a neon pink track jacket. I started to realize that it might be unusual that I was traveling alone to this place.

"Where are you from?" they asked me.

"New York. Where are you from?" I've lived so many places that saying I'm from New York doesn't feel accurate. The person looked at me with an expression I couldn't read behind their reflective sunglasses. Then they answered.

"South Dakota. I came to visit family and see this. I heard they wouldn't let us out of our cars because of COVID."

"I didn't know that. Where did you find out?" I asked. How close could we get by car? Was I relieved? Worried?

"I read it somewhere," they said, laughing. They turned out to be wrong. But I wouldn't know until I got to the checkpoint. As we finished our conversation, the row of cars started edging forward like one long caterpillar. We said goodbye to each other, and I hopped back into the rental, closed the door, and rolled forward with my windows down.

The alfalfa was wet with morning dew. Suddenly, I remembered picking wildflowers with my grandfather in Vermont when I was a child. I could feel the yellow flowers in my hands, hear his voice. We were picking them for my grandmother from a vacant lot on their street in Bennington, where they retired. My grandmother would have been sick already, but I don't think I knew that then. The dead visit us this way, through the senses. My brain must have been reaching back to the familiar to deal with this strange new experience. But all the same, I felt like he knew I was there. I thought, for a split second, he was in the car with me. I felt like a part of him had been caught in time here, that I was going to be closer to him, to the story he kept inside of himself while he raised a family in New Jersey, worked as an electrician, retired to Vermont. He never spoke of the desert other than to say he'd been stationed at "White Sands," yet he put his WWII photographs in an album with a cactus design on the cover. We bunched black-eyed Susan's and Queens Anne's Lace, the Green Mountains rolling above us. When grass smells a certain way, he visits me.

At the ID checkpoint, an unmasked military officer — a short man in aviator glasses — impatiently waved me forward and leaned into my window.

"You gotta keep going," he said, as I slowed and showed him my driver's license.

"The fog looks beautiful," I said, compelled to say something innocuous. He practically rolled his eyes at me. To be fair, I would have, too.

There should have been a ranch house — the McDonald Ranch House — open to the public that day with more photographs and displays. The McDonald Ranch House, which belonged to a rancher removed from his property with the promise he could return, was where the plutonium bomb was prepared before it exploded. However, at the checkpoint, the military officer gave me a pamphlet that said the ranch house display was closed "unfortunately due to unforeseen circumstances."

You drive through grasses and creosote and yellow wildflowers, all backlit by the rising sun, the edges catching the light and almost looking blue. As you get closer to where the access road turns off for the blast crater, what looks like fog — some of it — turns silver. I realized that what I thought was fog was some of the white gypsum sand that gives the White Sands Missile Range its name, as well as the name of the nearby White Sands National Monument.

Eventually, you come to an orange-vested military personnel member waving you to the left again. Drive, drive. My pulse started to quicken.

Then, a field where about twenty US Army officers in uniform and carrying enormous guns guide you to the exact spot where you can park your car, even how far to pull in. I was reminded of the precision with which the USAF operated the Pfizer vaccine distribution at Medgar Evers College — exactly where we stood in line, when we moved, where we sat, how we bared our arm of choice for the needle.

Once you park, you can stroll to the edge of the chain-link fence which you realize is a single, enormous circle enclosing what looks like nothing.

Fastened to the fence are yellow signs.

And before you walk inside the opening in the circle, you can stand at a table where there is a trinitite display. And there are some food vendors — stainless steel chafer pans like at a hotel hot breakfast. Who catered the Trinity Nuclear Blast Site buffet? I didn't stop to find out more, though people had already started lining up with paper plates. Cacti with flat petals grew along the fence edge — prickly pear. A white butterfly with black markings like calligraphy landed on the fence and fluttered off.

I walked through the opening into the fence and onto the site, looking down, pausing to notice my boots in the soil. I saw ants carrying what I thought were the bodies of dead insects into their holes.

Excitement was in the air. More and more people arrived wearing T-shirts and sneakers, light jackets. Masks on, masks off. Once people arrived inside the fence, they strode to ground zero, stepping carefully over the long grass and bumpy dirt. A black obelisk cast a long shadow in the sun. People leaned against it, posed for photos, smiling. I couldn't bring myself to get close to the structure. It looked sinister to me. And the violence it marked — my brain blocked it, though I tried to connect the spot of the blast to all of the death and poison it wrought.

At first, I judged the people who leaned against the obelisk and smiled. But as the minutes gathered, and I stood in the sunlight, I couldn't judge them. In such a difficult place, we respond how we can. I do not know anyone else's story. I do not get to say how anyone processes being here, in this impossible, dangerous, forbidden place.

"This bomb was the same one dropped on Nagasaki," a college-aged woman excitedly tells the group of people with her. "A different kind of bomb was dropped on Hiroshima." I recognize the lilt in her voice — she could be from the town where I taught for four years in the mountains of New Mexico. Or near the Raton pass into Colorado. But I did not know her.

I had already realized the bombs were the same. My grandfather was here and also involved with Nagasaki. At the Nuclear History Museum in Albuquerque yesterday, I started to see the gaps in the story, the holes in the fence. So much information is available about the Trinity Atomic Test Site, about the Hiroshima and Nagasaki bomb. But more so about the Hiroshima bomb crew, process, and plans. Much less about the Nagasaki bombing mission.

When you are at the fence of a classified event, you look for places that the wind has tugged at the wire, opening a hole the eye can peer into.

We had walked into the fence, past the Geiger counters people brought to the edge that were beeping wildly as though we were in a movie about coming here. We scattered and dragged our feet over the earth. We were inside the forbidden place.

The wind takes the things back that we borrow, I tell my child. I left her sleeping in her bed in a city on the coast where rain delayed my flight. The ash leaf or asphalt stone once in her warm hand. Look again — gone. She cries about this less now. And in autumn, like this first weekend in October, the trees begin to let go of pieces of themselves.

The wind takes away what it helped shape. Light, water, air. Minerals and dust.

We are all stardust.

A person sleeping in bed next to you emits more radiation than a small trinitite stone, I read, reassuring myself that night.

That afternoon, directly from the hotel after the nuclear test site, I drove to the Balloon Fiesta Park, parked in a huge lot, walked in the heat of the day where sky divers would fall from the clouds. People sat

on the ground and in folding chairs eating french fries and burritos.
I bought a burrito, and the green chili dribbled down my arm while I
found a sliver of shade draped over the dry dirt behind a vendor tent.

I heard murmurs, and then "Oh!" and three people — little cutout
shapes — dangled in the air, one holding an American flag. They
appeared to dance as they fell. Their parachutes tilted and flung them
sideways. They lived in the sky, in the blue. The flag rippled and then
bunched up. Then they fell, down, down, tumbling back to the earth.

✤ ✤ ✤

My grandfather lied about his war record, a man — a Facebook
"friend" — messaged me after *Hawk Parable,* the book of poems
that began my broader investigation into my grandfather's story, was
published. The man implied my grandfather lied, too.

When so much is online now, why don't you know more? is
a question I've been asked again and again, sometimes with more
suspicion than others. And *Can't you just find a veteran who was
there and ask them about it?* These questions do not acknowledge
the complexity of the secrecy surrounding the Manhattan Project, the
culture of silence around it, the classification of a lot of information
about it, even now, and the fact that very few veterans of the Second
World War are still alive.

All the same, *Why can't I find the answer about his involvement?*
I asked myself for years before I realized that his bomb wing number
meant more than I thought it meant. For years, I thought, if I
searched hard enough, I would be able to read a tidy story about his

actions. If only I could look more closely at a USAF database, tug at
the right archival document. If only the *USAF Heavy Bomb Group
Markings & Camouflage, 1941 – 1945* revealed what I needed. If only
I could locate the airplane serial number from one of my grandfather's
photos. The summer before my trip to the Trinity Site, I sat in the
famous Rose Main Reading Room piling military texts from the
General Research Division in front of me. I perched between spot 717
and 715 on the long oak table — slightly between numbered seats —
where light spilled onto the cloth-bound books from gaps between
skyscrapers outside the open window. I wanted to sit in the light, and I
wanted the light to touch these texts. I scoured the *B-29 Bibliography*.
I read everything I could about the 20th USAF, which I learned even
now has the sole purpose to "Defend the United States with combat
ready nuclear forces; on order, conduct global strike." The other day,
the *New York Times* published an article with the headline that
asserts, "As Russia Digs In, What's the Risk of Nuclear War? It's not
Zero." There has been a run on potassium iodide. A nuclear war would
immediately activate the 20th USAF, which in 1945 contained the
fleet of planes in the Hiroshima and Nagasaki bombing. My grandfather's bomb group was part of the 8th USAF, which confused me
for years. The "Mighty Eighth," as it was known, fought the Nazis in
Europe. My grandfather was never stationed or flew planes in Europe.
Not Germany, not France, not England. I thought I had the wrong
records. But that wasn't the case at all. I had everything right. And the
story connects back to New Mexico.

While I write this, I keep waiting for the National Personnel
Records Center to send me my grandfather's military records, which I

requested many months ago. The bomb and squadron numbers come from my great-aunt Bertha's address book, which my grandfather saved his whole life and gifted to my mother. Is the 6 really an 8? What does "b.w." mean? I researched rankings — groups, squadrons, and wings.

He was stationed in Alamogordo, New Mexico.

The last address for my grandfather — where mail could be sent when he was in the Pacific Theatre — lists him as being part of the 316 b.w. — bomb wing.

By accident, a page of a congressional hearing popped up in an intensive Google search I conducted and offered information about the 316th bomb wing. Some congressional hearings can be requested at major research libraries like the New York Public Library in New York City. There, I requested another document, *Hearings before the Special Committee on Atomic Energy, US Senate, Seventy-Ninth Congress, First Session, sr. 179, Part 1.* This hearing is in the database, but when I requested it, another text arrived at the desk. The wrong one.

When I asked a research librarian about this, she said, "Now hold on a minute, this is interesting. The system says it's here, but I also can't find it..." She raised her eyebrows, left the desk, then came back with another librarian. Both looked at the screen.

"You're right. You can't find it," the other librarian said. "But the computer says it's here."

A week before this, my first day at the library, after I scooped up my tower of military books and gingerly carried it across the polished floor to the sunny spot at the oak table, I sat down facing the entrance. A nondescript woman who looked like she was wearing a badge walked in, took out her phone, pointed it in my direction, took a photo quickly, and left. Was she taking a photo of me? I felt paranoid wondering this. But the question still came to mind.

As I sat at the table, the extent of my grandfather's story dawned on me. I felt my stomach flip and my cheeks get hot. I looked around the Rose Main Reading Room and adjusted the N95 mask I'd been re-wearing and that now smelled like mint gum. When I would take it off later, I'd see a smear of strawberry ChapStick inside the synthetic fibers. Only a few other people sat scattered at the long tables. When someone shuffled a backpack or slid a stack of books away or typed on a laptop, the little sounds congregated into small echoes. That was the moment I realized I hadn't been able to uncover my grandfather's story because it was still a redaction. I wasn't some kind of hack or a "bad researcher" who just couldn't find the right text. My imposter syndrome had been looming over me, telling me I wasn't a scholar, I wasn't a writer. Maybe I had cooked up this whole thing, it was saying. But then, it all came together.

He didn't lie.

And I would never know the story definitively. But I could come as close as I could.

The reason the information could not be found? The reason is that it never would be. It was still classified. *Even now.*

But why? Why now, when so much of the Second World War is in museums, in archives, open to the public? The reason is that something almost happened. Something terrible. Something that would have changed the history of the world.

My grandfather's words rang in my ears from the day he handed my mother the photo album. *This is classified,* he'd said. The word sounded melodramatic to me. Especially since embedded in the album were some photos of my grandfather and his friends posing with young women. *Classified? Really?* I couldn't take what he said seriously. But I did now.

In the report I discovered by sheer luck during some googling, in the PDF single page of the *Research and Development for Defense Hearings Before the Committee on Science and Astronautics, US House of Representatives, Eighty-seventh Congress, First Session,* I learned more about the General of the 316th bomb wing. Two years before the Trinity bomb test in the New Mexico desert, a General Roscoe C. Wilson "was appointed AAF Project Officer to support the Manhattan Engineering Division." More importantly is what comes next. My jaw dropped when I read it.

"In this post, he was one of the first officers involved in the development of the atom bomb. He chose the site of the first test (Alamogordo)."

The man in charge of the bomb wing my grandfather was part of — the bomb wing about which there is very little information — and that was stationed in the White Sands desert and then the Pacific Theatre chose the exact spot where the first atomic bomb would detonate. Seven months before the atomic explosion, he became "chief of staff of the 316th bomb wing."

My grandfather poses in the dark and in the sun in front of a jeep labeled with his nickname and "316 b.w." This is the jeep he took out into the gypsum dunes and drove into the endless and disorienting stretch of white sand.

There is a distinct rhetorical pattern to the lies the military told about the Manhattan Project. Information will either be removed or the very opposite of the thing that happened is stated with a negation. Over time, these negations of truth build one upon the next into a shadow story. The true story. Impossible to prove but all the same what you see when you peer through the hole in the fence. In the records and rosters I've seen, I have not found the 316th bomb wing. I've found the 315th. But not his.

The very day of the Trinity atomic explosion, the 8th USAF — the "Mighty Eighth" that many argued won the war in Europe — was reassigned to the Pacific Theatre "without personnel or equipment," I read.

The 316th bomb group was part of the 8th USAF.

I have photographs of my grandfather at the base in Okinawa, a haunted look in his eyes. On the back of one photo, I read scrawled in pencil, in shaky handwriting, *I've seen enough.*

The general in charge of deciding the location of the atomic bomb test was also in charge of a bomb wing of pilots. The bomb test was for the same bomb as the one *Bockscar* dropped on the city of Nagasaki. The pilots of the Hiroshima and Nagasaki blasts were never in New

Mexico. But the 316th bomb wing was. Those pilots — if my grandfather witnessed the bomb blast, and I think he did — would have seen what the bomb could do. Those pilots were part of another plan and yet the same plan. They had the knowledge of the fire. Of the light. Of all it could destroy. Of all it could take away.

✛ ✛ ✛

At the atomic bomb site, a mother and father push a stroller with rubber wheels over the bumpy, radioactive soil. A baby sleeps in the stroller clutching a lamb stuffy sewed to a pacifier. A toddler with cornsilk hair runs around the meadow grass with a matchbox car tucked into his palm. His father wants him to pose near the fence.

I overhear a guide from the White Sands Missile Range Museum — a man in a floppy green hat — tell someone that no, the fence doesn't look like that because of the blast. It's just the high desert winds that caused the fence to wear and rip.

I thought of my grandfather, lined up with other men his age. Not even twenty. His glance backward at the photographer who was recording the event — the proud generals posing in front of rows and rows of men in uniform in the desert lined up facing the mountains — is like a little gap in the fence. His gaze out and through it all, through history. He is seen and also sees the staging of spectatorship. His eyes say, *What am I doing here?*

"Grab it, look at me!" the father calls to his son with the blond hair the wind ruffles up from his forehead. The father is in tourist mode.

He wants his toddler to pose. To pose at the atomic test site. He wants his son to look at the camera lens — the lens on his phone.

The boy is not in tourist mode. The boy does not want to pose. But the boy does look at him, for a moment. Then breaks down and sobs in the sun and turns away, his back to the obelisk that marks ground zero.

I watched this scene, thinking about what it means to bring a child to a radioactive blast site. My brain couldn't get far with this musing. I had no answers other than the question itself as I watched this scene. I imagined my toddler here, picking flowers. I missed her. And I was so glad she would never come to this terrible place.

Now the toddler I observed was hungry, hot. He wanted his mother, who was holding his baby sister in her arms. She ignored him. "Stop crying," the father said. The boy would not stop crying.

The sobs, softened in the wind, were the only expression of sorrow I heard. I thought I would weep. But instead, I was stunned, along with the crowd. We had entered the fence, the forbidden place. And we were enchanted.

✛ ✛ ✛

An enchantment is a kind of distraction. You do not see the reality around you. You see something else, something that seems like it's from another place, another time. It becomes real — tangible. The product of someone else's will, someone else's design.

Standing at ground zero of the first nuclear explosion — the event that marked the era of ruin — comes close to the feeling of being in a

sacred space. That is the only way I can describe my expectation of
what it would feel like to encounter such an otherworldly energy. This
invisible presence that lingers from the thing that could destroy all life.

Maybe you are a spiritual person. You believe in a deity or deities:
God, G-d, Jesus, Mohammed, Brahman. Something else — or something
more personal. If you enter a sacred space, a temple, a church, a
mosque, a cemetery, you might feel a presence, if you have this belief.
The breath of life in what has been life. Energy. But love.

Maybe you aren't sure what to believe. Maybe you aren't spiritual.
I don't know what to believe, and sometimes I tell people I have a
productive relationship with doubt. I was raised Christian (loosely).
My spouse is Jewish. We observe Christian and Jewish holidays.
When I feel like I've lost my faith and I enter a nineteenth-century
Episcopalian church a block from where I live and walk up the steps
stained with soot and enter the cold darkness for a candlelight sound
bath service at sundown, and when I push away the superstructure,
close my eyes, and see the eyeball of the moon in my eyelids, I think
about the fingertips that have rubbed the pew my palms now hold.
The generations of mice that tunnel in and out of the foundational
stones. The dramatic pink and red lights of the ambulances catching
the lead-paned glass blues of saints in robes. The energy within
repetitive acts: the weekly entering and exiting. The daily journey
that shadows play over the dim room. The repetitive actions crafting
a kind of design. Like when we light our menorah as the days become
darkest, bringing more light, candle by candle, day by day into the
room. Some days, I believe nothing, others everything. When my
doubt fades, I feel love so palpable it's like having someone wrap their
arms around me.

The word my mind tried to find that morning the sky shifted from pink to pale blue in the field in New Mexico on a military weapons test site was "spiritual" — before I entered the blast radius and experienced the mesmerizing emptiness. Instead of being in the presence of the sacred, I felt like I was experiencing an enchantment as I stood in the chain-link ring marked with "Keep Out" signs. This is the best way I can describe it. The circle enclosing everything wrong. A will to be God. A will to destroy. I wasn't in the presence of love. I was in the presence of evil, and it mesmerized me, mesmerized all of us — that eternity we could glimpse, eternity created by humans through a power we cannot fathom.

When I stepped into the fenced circle, I planned to pray. But the prayer disappeared from my lips, and I felt stunned. I could not think. What is this place? What is this thing I feel? A part of the earth that looks like other parts of the earth surrounding it. But forbidden. Dangerous.

But also, a simple circle in the earth. A place where life perseveres — which is the gift of creation. The earth's gift to grow and cleanse itself in spite of all we put into it. Maybe this is why I couldn't see the way the prayers fell from my lips. Stunned, yes. I was stunned. To be here. To be in community here. To witness the place where such a plan for destruction began. To put the tread of my boots on the marked place and therefore leaving myself here. And also making myself vulnerable in doing this — to my own role in all of this, somehow. To my connection to the very young man from New Jersey whose parents didn't speak English and who passed a special test to be here. And to become a killing machine like the other children of war.

Teenagers in ripped black jeans and soft brown hair cut in angles across their eyes knelt in front of me. They rubbed their silver and maroon painted fingernails over the brownish orange dirt. They sifted the green and glassy trinitite from the ground with their fingers. Touched the glassy rocks the bomb created when it flashed. Fat red ants burrowed the glittery balls of it down into their holes. Then the insects brought the little chips and balls of it up again, to the surface.

"Oh, oh, oh!" an older woman gasped, staring at the ground. "Isn't she beautiful?" she breathed, mesmerized. Her fingers glittered in huge rings. She also bent to the dirt and touched it with her fingernails, sifting the dust for the green radioactive stones.

I don't want to insert myself here, even now, in memory. I want to forget that I visited this place, closed off from all other places with a circular fence. That I, too, fell under its spell.

I, too, looked down, down, down. I, too, bent over. I saw a piece of black and green that looked like a shard of light — of the absence of light, of the absence of all things — as though it had been waiting for me at the bottom of a pond in the woods. It looked like water. It looked like a tiny piece of absence — something that reminded me that all could be taken away in an instant.

Immediately, I felt horror.

That morning in Albuquerque, when I stood in the hotel hallway at the edge of dawn at five a.m. when the sky shifted from purple to orange, I glanced out the window as I waited for the elevator and checked my face mask to make sure it pressed against my nose. I could see three enormous hot air balloons in the sky. Red, blue, yellow.

Ding! the elevator had rung. An older woman with her mask slipping down below her nose stepped in. I held my breath, and we descended together. *Ding!* We both exited: I exited out the back hallway to the parking lot to visit an atomic test site, and she went to the front desk with its basket of apples and coffee carafe to wait for her group and go to the Balloon Fiesta.

That morning, as I left the parking lot in my rental car, globes were drifting above the Starbucks and Burger King like giant thought balloons over the terracotta dirt, the zero-scaped land at the curb of the strip mall scattered with gray stones instead of grown in with grass. Below the balloons, a tree here or there had been planted decoratively to cast thin shadows between the curb and highway. The balloons rose and would land. The balloon fiesta crowd of close to 800,000 people came that second autumn of the pandemic and would cheer at the launch. The sky would be so open and blue. The balloons put there by us, filled with gas, rising above the city at dawn, reminded me of question marks, three of them, tethered to individual and separate questions I could not locate below them on the ground.

So, the air smelled sweet. Morning lilies opened their orange trumpets at the edge of the road.

When I entered the fence with radioactive warnings fastened to the chain of metal, I wondered if I should I touch the obelisk marking ground zero. Should I? People lined up to pose next to the dark stones, grazing it with their shoulders, patting it with their palms. Wildflowers went to seed at the fence. The fence surrounding us becoming a radius. My left leg tingled, my sciatica from giving birth, but in that moment, the nerve pain felt like something more. My boots dragged through the long grass, scuffing it. Basic facts of the bombings were being recounted to groups of people. *Little Boy. Fat Man. Trinity was a Fat Man bomb — the Nagasaki bomb.* I caught the scraps of facts — very basic facts, the data points along the historical arc we've all told ourselves about this story — tumble from the lips of women and men, nonbinary teens and adults. I watched another solo traveler glancing at us with worry in their eyes. Like mine. The military cleared the rattlesnakes that morning — threw them with sticks outside the fence.

As people began bending down, touching the earth, you might think that they were praying. Stooping, bowing heads.

But everyone was scouring the earth for treasure.

And in the midst of it all, there were porta-potties outside the fence, lined up in Crayola-colored plastic. Grasshopper wings clacked under the crowd's murmur. I trekked through the grass. Alfalfa smelled sweet, like Vermont, and I again remembered picking wildflowers with my grandfather in Bennington. I decided to walk the radius and say a prayer. *I'm sorry. Forgive us all. Let us learn,* I began to say into my N95 mask.

The US military had hung foam posters printed with reproduced photos of the blast, plus some of military police on horseback the week of the test in 1945. This was the strangest museum exhibit I had ever witnessed and probably will ever witness. And here, in a photo, Oppenheimer and Groves stood, famously, at the twisted remains of the bomb tower. It seems impossible they were here. But they were.

I kept thinking about how on July 16, 1945, a day before the US military reassigned the "Mighty Eighth" USAF forces from the European Theatre to the Pacific Theatre, scientists authorized the first detonation of an atomic bomb. The very next day, the 316th bomb wing — my grandfather's bomb wing, part of the Mighty Eighth now — was assigned to the Pacific Theatre.

Close to hundreds and hundreds of thousands of people congregated that weekend in the hot, dusty park an hour and a half away where every October since the '70s enormous, heat-filled globes floated and lifted up high into the air. Busloads of people arrived in my hotel every year for the International Balloon Fiesta. I was lucky to find a room. While I stood inside the circumference of an atomic explosion, breakfast burritos and fry bread were being sizzled on grills as the sun rose, as the balloons lilted in the wind above the crowd not far from there. Snoopy and Sponge Bob, striped and checked like NASCAR flags filled the sky with color an hour and a half from the point on the earth that had once exploded a momentary sun.

The globe of fire that was here, too, lifted high into the earth. Its own balloon. At least for the second of time that cameras collected the shape on film. Cracking like an egg. Rolling up, curling, shooting skyward, building and building — shapes that were nearly impossible to perceive and describe as they shifted — then showering radioactive dust northeastward across New Mexico.

To be enchanted is to be caught inside the circle of someone's design — a design with no beginning or end. A design that only serves the self that made it and that self's values, greed. The magic is powerful. For months afterward, the grassy circle within the fence appeared in my dreams. I would bring my child to the fence and wake up just as I said, No! Sometimes, I stood inside the fence alone, wondering even in my dream why I was there.

A part of me would always be inside that circle.

A white butterfly nursing on the milkweed paused near a gap in the nuclear test site fence.

All of a sudden, after I bent down, forgetting the prayer on my lips and stared at the ground.

And then, then, I fled — out of the circle, past the crowd, the food vendors, the porta-potties with their sour smell, the soldiers with guns, to my car. Then I drove to the edge of the checkpoint, where cattle touched their wet nostrils to the long grass as they wandered onto the White Sands Missile Range. Then past the downwinders protesting the bomb and the illness it brought to their families. Then to the town of San Antonio, New Mexico, with its "original" Owl Bar and Café being the closest place to grab a bite to eat after visiting the blast site. I did not go there.

My boot pressed down on the gas and the car lurched past it as I flew down the empty highway, away from it all afterward. Faster, faster. The car bucked over a hill. And then there was Socorro, New Mexico — a McDonald's. I swerved into the parking lot, dashed inside, waited in line to buy coffee and clear my head from the panic it was stuffing down my throat and to my heart.

It was the teenager working the register's first day on the job. He couldn't figure out how to open the cash drawer. I told him about my first day using a cash register while I stood there, breaking into a sweat and panicking.

I held the cup in my hands while my boots walked dust from the site onto the tiled floor — to the glass door and out into the bright sun.

The scent of thin french fries turned my stomach. The air still smelled like them in the parking lot. I had begun to break apart.

Back in the car, I checked my phone.

Touch your jeans with your hands, my therapist texted me. *Breathe.*

My jeans felt soft, and I touched the tiny yellow stitches at the seam. I'd scrubbed my hands raw. But it felt comforting to touch my body and feel my own warmth, my own presence, and return to myself.

Until I stood there, inside the test site, I had a hard time realizing that this was a real place — even though I had been studying this place for years, lived not far from it, danced to bands who played in the city an hour and a half away before having a baby and then moving to New York. We stayed in that same hotel where I woke that morning to hot air balloons tethered in the dark when we lived two hours away in the mountains and wanted to go out in Albuquerque.

I've only been to temple once, but I remember a prayer as a *thank you,* G-d, for the gift of the sun in the morning and its dip below the earth in the evening. Thank you, each day, for the gift of this earth. There is life, even here, in this ruined place. Thank you to the creator for the mind you've given me to perceive these things. For the shadows in the story. For the gaps in the fence. And for the green and white roots that gather there, bringing life back.

I imagine my footprints inside the bomb crater — that they'd still be there, the treads, as though I left them on the windless surface of the moon.

But the marks my soles left would be gone within a few hours
in the wind that barrels between the mountains on the missile range.
The fence between the former bomb crater now grown in with grass
and wildflowers and the rest of the active military explosives test site
ripples as though by a shock wave, as though by a bomb. But no —
and not by hands pulling and pulling on it, or by pliers cutting through
the wire and twisting it open.

I don't quite have the tools to cut the fence, but I'm here, looking
through it.

31. *Site:* Snow in July

The following works are visual essays. They are erasures. They are
stains. They re-print the indentation that the Trinity bomb blast
smashed into New Mexico's soil. If someone else were to write an
object label for these works (if they were hanging on a wall in a
gallery), this is what the square of text might say:

Site is a four-part series of visual poems / essays / works.
Each work reproduces the Trinity Test site in New Mexico
— the location of the first atomic blast the world has known —
at specific moments in time after the detonation. The works,
titled to reflect this, are "0.016 Seconds," "0.053 seconds,"
"2.0 seconds," and "28 hours." Part pencil drawings of
photographs taken by cameras scientists *hoped* would
capture the blast without being destroyed by the explosion,
part gestural water color paintings, part collages of computer
punch cards used by the Los Alamos National Laboratory
during the height of the atomic age, and part erasures of eyewitness observations of the site shortly after the radioactive
burst boiled and cooled, these mixed-media expressions
of time, place, and military-driven environmental trauma
intend to invite the viewer / reader to think about the self in
relation to history, the environment, the body, and ways of
experiencing the catastrophic.

Instead of a de-personalized description, I'm trying to put into
words what it was like to make these works. And why I've made them.
Why do I want the viewer to look closely at instead of away from

a shape that signals horror? What is at stake if we look away, if we assume we already understand what there is to know?

No one knows fully what there is to know about this subject because the complete story about it has been partially hidden from the beginning. But I invite you to perceive the origins of the horror, even in the limited way we have of understanding it.

✢ ✢ ✢

I sketched and collaged these pieces at a residency outside of Chicago in the last trimester of a pregnancy. I couldn't believe I was chosen to attend. There, I was even given my own artist studio. But the trip was hard on me. All the same, I went. I didn't have the space to make the visual works I had in mind in my apartment in Santa Fe.

One of the other residents, a performance artist, would eat the avocados and apples I shuffled on foot to the grocery store to buy, stuffed in my backpack, and then labeled in the communal fridge. "Oh, these were yours?" she'd ask, the baggie with my name on it in Sharpie sitting on the counter.

Hungry, stretched out, and exhausted, I bent over the studio table and steadied my hand. To draw a shape, I'd break it down in my mind into smaller and smaller shapes. The cloud became a sweeping curve. The dust became ruffles of triangles and smaller triangles. I did not like looking at these details. I felt everything I knew disappearing into geometry.

I created these works while I lived in New Mexico but three and a half years before I would visit the atomic test site.

In these works, I included erasures of eyewitness observations of the site shortly after the radioactive burst boiled and cooled. These eyewitness observations I included came from scientists who knew what they were seeing. Photographers staged the cameras that took the photos these drawings are based off without knowing if the cameras would be destroyed by the explosion. Both the reproductions of the cloud and the utterances about it came from observers with inside knowledge of what this cataclysmic explosion was.

Photographers did not think about the ranchers, community members, and children nearby, who would have no idea what was coming. Who would not understand the earth-shaking sound, the blast of light.

The job of the photographer was to capture the never-before experienced blast. Photographic lenses trained on the site, nothing more. No one involved gave a thought to the Indigenous and Hispanic communities living off the land. Outside the frame. Erased from this moment that would change everything. I want these works to invite a kind of looking that acknowledges this violence. The violence of overlooking. Of forgetting. Of erasing.

The following works, which I sketched from photos taken of the atomic cloud in moments of time after the blast, are titled "0.016 Seconds," "0.053 seconds," "2.0 seconds," and "28 hours." The bubble expanding, expanding, expanding, and then a scar.

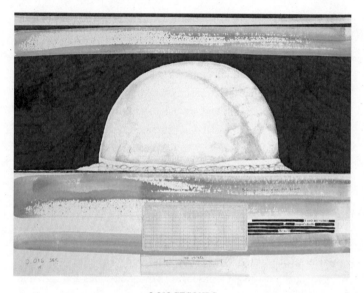

0.016 SECONDS

When I lived and taught in New Mexico, I met one of the Tularosa Basin Downwinders, whose family got cancer in the months and years following the blast and was left out of the Radiation Exposure Compensation Act (RECA) that offered funds for downwinders of the nuclear tests the US conducted in other parts of the American Southwest. But New Mexicans, impacted by the very first test, the then-secret blast a month before the devastating decimation of two cities in Japan and murder of Japanese citizens, had at that time been ignored.

I thought about the Tularosa Basin Downwinders as I hand-drew the Trinity Test site, where the first atomic blast the world has known exploded in New Mexico, at specific moments in time after the detonation. I think about how their stories have been so often left out of this representation of the event.

✛ ✛ ✛

When I dragged my paintbrush over the paper, I despaired, thinking that the color and streaks looked amateurish. The brush speckled the page. I thought about a robin's egg. The stakes felt so high to me, to take on this subject visually. I wanted my intent to be perceived. I forbid any of the artists from entering my studio for studio visits.

Until the final week, when the works were finished.

Before I made these works, I'd had two miscarriages, one which led to an ER visit and an emergency D&C, a procedure which is not protected any longer unilaterally in the US now that the Supreme Court overturned *Roe v. Wade*.

When I was making these works, I was also researching hospitals in the Chicago area in case the baby came early. I'd traveled from New Mexico, where I was living, to make these pieces. No one could talk me out of going. I knew I was fortunate to be able to attend. I finished grading finals in the studio while glue was drying between pieces of paper on the collages. New mothers aren't often at residencies because children are forbidden, and I didn't know what the future would bring. I already felt strange, bringing myself and the growing other inside of me, to the residency.

✢✢✢

After I made these works, I bled, hoping I'd make it back to New Mexico for the birth. I sat in a metal chair one night under the track lighting of the studio with my cell phone pressed to my ear. I was on hold, waiting for the nurse on call in Santa Fe to advise me about the amount of blood I'd found in my underwear.

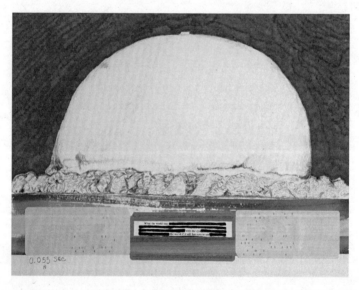

0.053 SECONDS

I chose pink for this visual work — a wrong pink. I soaked the paper around my drawing of the atomic cloud growing over the New Mexico desert at 0.053 seconds after the detonation with a pink that is only found in certain flower petals. Or in plastic toys. It's the color of a highlighter you might choose to illuminate words you want to recall later. The perforations marking data let color into the cards like tiny windows.

Photographers protected the cameras that took the photos of the first atomic cloud in a bunker, hoping the equipment would not be destroyed by the explosion. Representations we have now of the cloud caught in time from one nanosecond to the next as it spread do not reflect what a witness could perceive and try, impossibly, to describe.

When I started these works, I wanted the viewer to pay attention, to look at what the human eye could not understand, as the shape of the cloud changed so quickly that the brain would not recognize these individual shapes. Instead, a witness would leave with an impression.

The mushroom, yes, but not the incremental changes. The brain could not register these in time.

During the studio visit at the end of the residency, another performance artist — not the person who ate my food — pointed at my rounding stomach, then the artwork, and said, "Look, you're drawing yourself!"

I could see what they saw. A rounding swell. Like my own torso. As the days progressed, the fetus grew so much that I had a hard time keeping up with my fellow residents after dinner on evening walks. I lagged behind.

Why had I created this cloud so that it looked like a human body? I wondered later. The bleeding would stop. I would keep the fetus inside my uterus until I went back to New Mexico for her birth.

On July 16, 1945, fallout 250 miles long and 200 miles wide blanketed New Mexico. It looked like snow. The fluffy flakes carpeted cattle and crops. The very next year, the infant mortality rate was fifty-six percent higher than the year before.

SITE 2.0 SECONDS

Two seconds after the detonation, there was darkness, a purple light. In "Site 2.0 Seconds," I redacted an eyewitness account so that it reads, "the ominous cloud hanging over us / brilliant purple / radioactive glowing / it just seemed to hang / there forever."

That cloud would, in a sense, hang there forever. Invisible. But haunting the sky. And touching the people who live there with its wrong energy.

I chose punch cards that kept track of "property records" at the Los Alamos National Laboratory when atomic tests were being conducted in Nevada. I wondered what "property" was being accounted for. I wondered about the implications of the word, "property." The Manhattan Project claimed the land of the Tularosa Basin as its property. But the poison seeped out of it, impossible to contain. Unlike my infant born just over a two-hour drive from the north entrance to the Trinity Blast crater, the infants and children who sickened and died in New Mexico were among the first fatalities of nuclear weapons.

✛ ✛ ✛

Spectators of the cloud — and this very representation of it — had the privilege of its knowledge. Reproductions of the Trinity cloud are inscribed with this gaze. The gaze of the perceiver who witnesses an act of harm and knowingly keeps those nearby away from this knowledge. In making these works, I wanted the viewer to look closer, not away. To trace this gaze and understand it as a limitation. To contemplate the violence of this kind of looking and its role in our cultural reckoning with this historical event.

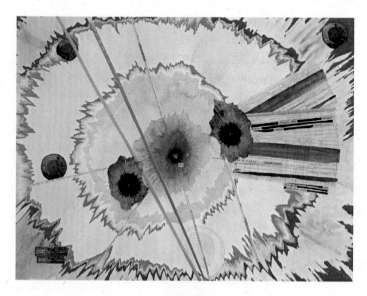

28 HOURS

Twenty-eight hours, a day later, a photographer sat in a plane and flew over the bomb crater. The final photos of the site are taken from the sky. From the place where the cloud had towered and dispersed.

What did the pilot and photographer think as they crossed that haunted air? That ghost tower? And looked down at the scarred soil?

Sometimes the mind doesn't have much space for more than marvel. Horror. Awe. Words can't always form in the mind as thoughts.

Animals like jackrabbits that happened to be in blast zone suffered and died.

As I sketched, painted, cut, and glued these works, I thought about whose perceptions of the first atomic detonation are not part of the public eye. Not reproducible as photographs. Not caught by camera shutters protected in an embankment.

Who experienced this world-ending destructive force and must be inscribed in it? What does it mean that now our sense of what happened at this site is shaped by imagery that erases the other witnesses, the people other-ed, kept from knowledge?

Children nearby rolled in the fallout and rubbed it on their skin that day as odd fluff drifted over the desert.

"Snow in July!" they yelled as they played in what fell. "Snow in July."

32. Bloom

"Is this Tyler Mills?"

"Yes?" I would confirm, my voice up-ticking. The sound of my voice would surprise me: I thought I had flattened the questions out of my statements.

"We have information for you about your grandfather. He was a very skilled pilot, and the USAF wanted him to train for a very special program ... " The voice on the other line would sound firm, clipped.

I would lean against the yellow wall in the kitchenette of the new apartment in Santa Fe and close my eyes. *Finally, a confirmation that he was part of the mission.* It would be like I had reached into a thorny bush and twisted off the stem of a single rose.

Batman and I had recently moved the afternoon of Halloween from the house we rented in a New Mexico ranching town to the small city of Santa Fe, an hour away. That day, the U-Haul Batman drove broke down in the mountains near the Glorieta Pass, and one of the cats took a runny shit in the car I was driving. As the sun disappeared into the trees and children began to put on skull masks, we settled into blankets swirling in the nests we made on the empty living room floor of our new apartment — exhausted but relieved.

A man had been stalking me at work, then appeared near the house where we had been living twice in one week. I filed a police report and documented evidence of what had been happening for the past three months, but Human Resources hinted that perhaps I had an odd fascination with the man, since I had a trove of information about his whereabouts. (How easily the narrative flips in a patriarchal system.) There is a whole other story in that experience, but for now, I want to say that this all happened when the cotton cobwebs you can buy at Walgreens stretched over the bushes of the houses on the street. Plastic spiders comingled in the wheel-shaped webs the orb-weavers spun in the corners of doorways. The designs glowed in streetlamps, blooming with faint evening light — the real webs and the fictions indecipherable from one another. The gauzy scrim caught the light in chaos.

I had stepped into the murky stillness of the system that had put men in charge, and I mucked up the dirt. The more I tried to make things right, the more the cloudy liquid of it swirled around and around me in the water. I couldn't see my feet, or where to step next, though I did move away, finally. Even after that, I'd look in the rearview mirror as I drove to campus and from time to time see the man's truck behind me, tracing the lines my wheels made in the light powder of snow. *He's free to come and go. You can't prove this is about you.* HR's words echoed in my brain.

I would see the man every single time I left my office, left my classroom, left the building, walked to my car or walked home. He would key into my office without knocking when I was inside, give me earrings as I walked into the women's bathroom, fix his bicycle in the hallway during my night class, where I would see him every single time I'd be in the hallway, and then I'd see him again immediately afterward as he stood outside the building at nine p.m. watching me get into my car. He would be sitting on the park bench I'd pass on my walk home. He would be in the parking lot when I cut through campus to grab a cup of coffee. Every single time my body left the privacy of my office or my home or my car, I would see him, cross paths with him. He became a part of my day, my pattern, the landscape my body trafficked. Six, seven, eight, nine times a day. I didn't see anyone else in my life that often, not even Batman. After a while, I tallied the times I *didn't* see the man as though those were extraordinary occurrences. But most often, just as I'd note his absence, he'd appear right then, stepping out from around the corner of my street so we would cross paths — just as the notation of his absence had barely begun to scrape the green chalkboard of my consciousness.

Moving on Halloween seemed symbolic to me in some way. I didn't need the world to pretend to be frightening. I didn't need to go to a party where people dressed up in masks and Jack the Ripper cloaks with scythes or Zombie [insert-politician here], or Zombie [insert-celebrity here]. Our first night in the new place, Batman and I ate Snickers out of a plastic pumpkin head. The head would glow in the dark, and the candy sat inside it like gray matter in a lobotomized skull. No children came to the door.

The new kitchen couldn't fit a table, and one of the stove burners coiled cold under pots of spaghetti. But I liked the openness of it all. The kitchen opened to the dining area, which opened to the living room. I had lived in so many apartments with a layout like this one that the oldest cat — who had been with me for more than ten years — strutted over the carpeting as though she were coming home.

But I began all of this with a phone call — an imagined phone call. The first version of the call would confirm that my grandfather *had* participated in the Nagasaki mission. The phone call would confirm everything — my grandfather's story, his whereabouts, his atomic cloud photograph. But here is the second version — the other possibility.

The phone would ring, and I would lean against the couch facing the westward windows. I would look absently at the snow-tipped mountains. The animal haunches of the slanting peaks would smolder in the late afternoon. The clouds above them would look like they burned into the cave of evening to show us something about our ideal world.

"Is this Tyler Mills?"

"Yes," I'd say, punctuating the end of the word. I successfully flattened the uptick.

"We're calling on behalf of the US government regarding your story," the voice would say. "There are no records that your grand-father was part of the atomic missions in any way."

This phone call would mean that my grandfather didn't tell the truth, or that he had mislead me by accident, or that I incorrectly listened to his story, piecing the wrong patches of the past together. *Write true fiction,* he had told me once, at the end of his life. What did this mean?

To enter my new apartment complex, you have to punch a code in a box with metal numbers that feel pleasing under the fingertips — like flute keys. You can slip around the fence on foot, as I often did to head out to the Arroyo de los Chamisos Trail on my run.

"What is the gate code?" my friends would ask.

"The year World War II started," I'd text back.

"Then #."

+ + +

It is tempting to think that historical events become part of a global brain we can tap into with a few keystrokes, our fingers pressing down on the letters that would tell all the databases and search engines to open the world up for us like a bulb.

Inside, the petals would reveal the hip and anther. Inside the swirling corolla of the rose, you'd find nutlike seeds. You could warm them in your palm. Then you'd put them into soil. These seeds will rehearse for you the story of our making and unmaking: bulb, bloom, then seed again. Bulb, bloom, then seed again. Again. Again.

The problem with my story is that I feel like I hardly have one.

"It doesn't matter," Batman would say, sliding out of the black sleeves of his track jacket. "And you do have a story." His shape would cross the threshold, the shadows melting off of him and into the stairwell. The LED bulb in the frosted dome on the wall gave light to his form. He would take off his hat and became himself again. I became less and less of myself those days I spent creating myself on the page.

+ + +

The Manhattan Project still evokes redacted declassified documents — so much so that the image itself is almost a cliché. I might never find the answer to my question about my grandfather because it might never have even been recorded and archived. Why was my grandfather stationed in Alamogordo, New Mexico, where the Trinity Test exploded the first atomic bomb the world has known, before he shipped out at the end? Why did he say, "This was classified," when he gave his album of photos to my mother that contained an atomic cloud? Why did he say he was there that day? Why did he say he was interviewed to fly the mission? What happened — or didn't?

I've been rehearsing the possibilities for this story in a pink notebook covered with fuchsia roses I bought at Walmart my first month in the Southwest, in Las Vegas, New Mexico, where I had been living. Some of the blossoms look like they've been stenciled on. Some look like a teenager decoupaged the swirling petals on the cover. They bloom pinkly all over it. Inside, I would handwrite sentences like this:

> *I wanted to put my story — fragments, ruminations —*
> *about nuclear tests in a notebook like this one, I suppose,*
> *so I could have the luxury of feeling like a hobbiest —*
> *which to me always implied picnic baskets filled with*
> *sandwiches and wine and a box of watercolor wells and*
> *one paintbrush wrapped in cheesecloth.*

How funny that my brain went right to Manet paintings. How privileged this seems — art as leisure. For some reason I connected the idea of a hobby with a pre-twentieth century bourgeois ideal. I could sit in the park with my hot-pink spiral notebook and scribble my thoughts about the atomic blast (though I never did). "Free time" so often means picking up a second or third job — like Batman and I did for our debt — or sliding into the Technicolor baubles of gif memes on the cellphone screen, or checking work email, or closing your eyes and finally *(finally)* falling into sleep.

Choosing a notebook for a dollar or so has been one of my favorite ways to escape reality since I was twelve, when I would wander the aisles of the now-defunct Ames (Kmart's twin) when I lived in the North Country of upstate New York, close to the Canadian border, from ages eleven to eighteen. The purple, blue, cartoon-colored, wire-bound, or sometimes sewn, notebooks in the "Back to School" or "Paper Goods" aisle (depending on the season) held what seemed like a discovery, especially in the rural town where I spent half of my childhood dodging buckets of ice melt seeping from the ceiling and dripping down into trash cans in the halls of my school.

I bought notebooks like my new one covered in roses with babysitting money. At twelve, I bottle-fed infants parents dropped off at our house. I coaxed three-year-olds to pee before putting their boots on to play in the snow. I made three dollars an hour from one family until I got the courage to ask for a dollar raise. I cared for other children, a child myself.

Sometimes the notebook pages would stick together in the store, and there, the florescent light tinting the aisle with a religious aura, I'd crack the books open and flip the pages. *Blank, blank, blank, blank.* I'd put the nothing-yet back on the metal shelf after I had split the lark of it open.

Split the Lark — and you'll find the Music — Bulb after Bulb, in Silver rolled —

These notebooks, the ones where I would plan poems and short stories about women fighting their way out of the evil king's lair, needed lines that shone perfectly blue like a jay's cerulean wing. The spacing couldn't be too wide or the words would become too bubbled. Finding "college rule" paper with thinner, blank spaces between the lines, required patience. Stores always seem to carry fewer of these notebooks.

My words needed to loop like electrical wire around each horizon line the page offered. The sentence can skate over, and dip into, each new division of heaven and earth, sky and soil — down and down the page.

✢ ✢ ✢

The horizon guides pilots in flight and helps keep them from wiping out, even though instrument readings are crucial — often more crucial.

When thick clouds arrive, that is when disorientation becomes dangerous — even deadly. According to *The Killing Zone: How and Why Pilots Die:*

> Clouds and low visibility by themselves are not dangerous. But humans are not adapted to the loss of sensory perception that takes place inside a cloud. The challenge of instrument flight is to substitute the visible horizon with instruments that portray the horizon. While using instruments a battle rages inside the pilot's body. The proprioceptive and inner ear senses will continually try to convince the pilot's brain that motions and accelerations are

taking place that do not agree with the flight instruments.
The pilot must ignore what the body is saying and trust what
the instruments are saying — but this is very hard to do.

I think about what this battle between the body's sense of the
world and what the instruments convey to the intellect might mean
for all of the people who train as pilots and die during practice runs.

Fear is so often subjective, based on bias and misunderstanding.

I think about what an atomic bomb looks like when it lights up the lid
of the sky, stealing the horizon, whiting it out, destroying the creative
act that, in the tradition I grew up with, shaped the world.

> *Then God said: 'Let there be a firmament in the midst of*
> *the waters, and let it divide the waters from the waters.'*
> *Thus God made the firmament, and divided the waters*
> *which were under the firmament from the waters which*
> *were above the firmament; and it was so.*

And it was so. It *was,* says language. *Was.*

As a child, I remember thinking it was important to draw the
horizon line on the page, behind the house and the trees, so the sky
and the land, the sky and the water, separated.

Bloom suggests life, opening, and fertility. I am not a gardener, though I hope that can change. I have let many tomato plants scorch into pulpy husks on the fire escape of one of our old apartments in Chicago. But I recently planted seeds in planters, measuring the dirt with a pencil so I wouldn't bury them too deep. I have been waiting, hoping, to see sprouts peek out from the soil I have been keeping moist.

About roses, what I do know is that you need to deadhead the plant for more blooms. You "thumb prune" the bush, I read, so you get the big blooms, sacrificing the side buds that might be perfectly healthy. You cut away any downward-growing buds. You trim off the stems that cross one another as though they conveyed conflicting information. What survives? The moneymaker — yes, soft, sweet, sensual — that gathers the light in its petals and wins awards at rose shows. (Rose shows? Yes, rose shows.) In reading about roses, I've learned they're bisexual, that they bloom in strong sun, and that they can grow from seed in shallow trays after they've been cooled to break their pattern of dormancy. I've learned that many things can stress them out: mites, darkness, wind, and animals that rub the branches or pee over the soil that folds over the roots like chocolate cake batter.

When I was thirteen, a boy gave me a rose. I would put my lips to the bud and close my eyes to the lightly sweet scent. You feel like the inward curving petals are little lips kissing you back.

If you accidentally glance at the sun when you're driving and have nowhere else to look — try as you might to block the orb with your free hand — the afterimage you see looks like a bloom. A dark blotch that looks reddish to me, even velvety, before it disappears.

I took the wrong exit to our new apartment after driving through the mountains one evening. As the sun set, the sky became a tangerine peel, the blue clouds pulling through it. Part of the drive leads you directly west, so the coin of the sun glares at you, into your eyes, and the road lights up all orange, all gold, and you can only see a few feet ahead of you while you shield your eyes with a hand.

Finally, I thought I could turn off the highway and see the road ahead — how this was quickly becoming a metaphor — but the exit numbers blotted out, and the wrong ramp looped around to another road that beamed me directly into the low sun again. I tried to cup it with my left hand while I steered. I worried jellyfish blotches would start floating into my vision: indigo blue, blooming all over the curtain of my sight.

When I pulled into the parking lot, eventually, and switched off the engine that kept ticking in the dimming light, I imagined I could still see these shadow flowers.

Here is the bare fact of a bomber in a black-and-white photo. The Pacific light is so bright the men squint. They stand around it in the shadows of the huge metal body as a team. Together, they become a part of history for the person in the distance who holds the camera up, the lens glinting at them for a moment in the sun. My grandfather stands with them, darkness in his eyes. The shutter clicks.

I assume my grandfather gave this person his camera and asked for the photo so he could include it in the album where he kept his story: the tents where he slept, his friends — one kid in particular who looks even younger than my seventeen-year-old grandfather, and homesick. My grandfather stands with him protectively in a few shots.

I think of the side buds of the rose trimmed from the plant so the main bud can bloom fully. I think about narrative, how we fit history into it. I think about how my grandfather enlisted in the USAF too young, so he used a cousin's name for a year. This confuses the records. There are two versions of him in one database I could briefly access. I once wanted to "solve the mystery," his mystery, through my poems. But this was not possible — and not what poetry *does*, anyway. (Not for me, at least.) I think about how random archival information can be: what was saved, and why? Why was one manuscript not lost in the fire that destroyed all the others? Why was one record preserved and another shredded? Why was one event recorded and another not recorded? One trek into the past seemed to indicate that my grandfather was stationed in Germany for a time, even though he wasn't. He was stationed in the Pacific Theatre.

You trim off the stems that cross one another so the bloom grows bigger and bigger against a backdrop of leaves that almost frame it: inside is the thick green foliage of a past that was or never was.

How do we regard this past — this foliage thick with shadow and tight buds? What do we pinch off in service of a still life? At what point do we pluck the bloom we carefully made and lay it out on the butcher-block table next to a warm glass of white wine, a pewter candlestick tipped over, some green olives that look like they've been sucked on and spat out on the plate with their nutty pits still un-bit from the center? Does what we make become like a Dutch Golden Age Still Life? (*Never!* I imagine a snarky reader answering, as this imagined reader always does according to my inner critic.)

But I mean this: at what point are we peeling away the leaves from the thorns of history and composing something utterly symbolic from its materials — letters, a half-remembered story, a photograph, some incomplete or even mis-numbered records — and framing it for our purposes? When I write an essay, I aim at the truth like a hawk hunting the sandy brush for a mouse. I see them looking, these birds of prey, when I'm out running on the trail. We know that Michel de Montaigne titled his genre-breaking 1580 collection of nonfiction *Essais,* or "attempts." What are we expecting from nonfiction as it promises us a representation of reality, or the presentation of facts? The self holds all these things together and has to knock at the door, again and again, hoping the address is correct this time — but perhaps later, scribbling it down wrong. Perhaps you were never even exactly there to begin with when you wandered around lost in the rare rainfall that comes quickly in the desert. Maybe the rain never came, but was supposed to, and you could smell it like iron in a mineral spring.

Naming and metaphor intertwine: one suggests the literal, a label. The other suggests a transformation. But how does one become the other?

It wasn't until my grandmother — my pilot grandfather's wife — died that we learned her middle name, Rose, might not be Rose.

And my grandfather, when he met her, didn't give her his real name.

They met young, in a dancehall in North Jersey shortly after
the War. Was it springtime? Did the dancers dip ladles into bowls of
punch floating with sliced oranges and scoops of pink sherbet? How
did the red, white, and blue streamers twist through the exposed
beams of the ceiling? What did the live band play on their trumpets
and trombones? Did they dance first — or did my grandfather make
some wisecrack when he walked up to her? Did she walk up to him
and his friends while they stood outside smoking cheap cigars? What
did they say, or not say, as they waited for my grandfather's friend to
pull up in the car that my grandfather owned but pretended wasn't
his? Was that when he told her his name was Roger, when it wasn't,
because he wanted to seem like someone else? Where did "Roger's"
friend take them all in the car my grandfather bought with his electrician's salary? Was he proud to own something so ostentatious after
wearing his older sister's cast-off shoes all through school?
As he sat in the back bucket seat, did he put his arm around the
woman he would marry? Did they hold hands? Did they look in
opposite directions out the windows? Did he tell her his real name
after they kissed?

And why did my grandmother think her middle name was Rose?
Was it really Rose, or was it the different name printed on my mother's
birth certificate? After my grandmother died, my mother wore a little
rosebud on a chain (in rose gold) for her.

Pink, yellow, white — so many colors — of roses appear on seed
packets and in the gardening books I would look at in the library. But
why did my mother's birth certificate list another middle name? Why
did her brother's birth certificate list "Rose" as his mother's middle

name? What happened with these records? Why did it look like he and my mother had two separate mothers? My mother called the Department of Health in New Jersey to request a corrected version.

"Prove it," they said. "Prove that wasn't her name."

She couldn't.

✣ ✣ ✣

"Prove it," is what I keep hearing in my mind.

In one version of history, something happened. In another, it didn't — or not quite the way we can imagine, but rather in some murky area where the Manhattan Project cast rays of light over the road ahead so all that could be done is put one boot in front of the other, box up one more gadget to be shipped out, go on one more mission the day the sky explodes.

Photographs of the first atomic cloud at the Trinity site look like blossoms, blooms, but also jellyfish, cauliflower, cotton candy.

The cloud becomes these forms, and then a brain, before it dissolves.

Coda

Fire

On Friday the 13th, in January, an envelope appeared in the mail the size of a piece of paper folded in half. What was inside felt thicker than a single sheet of paper. I'd just swung open our apartment's black creaky door, kicking a winter boot out of my way so I could wipe my feet on the mat of the narrow entrance. Out of the shadows, Batman appeared. The darkness melted away in a flash as he switched on the hall light. My spouse blinked in the sudden brightness — he'd been working in the dark while the sun set — and handed me the envelope.

"Yay!" our daughter squealed, kicking off her shoes and rushing into the living room.

"Are you ready to open it?" he asked.

"Let me take off my coat first," I said.

I wasn't ready.

The letter was from the National Personnel Records Center, the "Agency Services" division of the National Archives. I stepped into the narrow hall and main room, placing the envelope on the table and shrugging out of the poof that was my winter coat. It slid down the back of the chair. Meanwhile, our toddler bounced toward me, then hugged my legs and flopped to the floor so I couldn't move. I reached down to help her wiggle out of her own puffy coat: pale pink hearts floated over her head. We'd been happy to discover this cheerful coat in the hand-me-down bag from her older friend. Once freed, our daughter screamed, scrunched up her nose, and ran to the couch, immediately yanking off all the cat-scratched cushions and shoving them onto the rug. She then stomped on the mound and roared.

"I'll open this in the kitchen!" I called, darting down the hall. I ducked into our galley kitchen separated from the living room / dining room with a solid wall with a square cut out. "Yes, you can watch — " I began, and the TV switched on. The cutout in the wall allows you to stand at the sink and peer out of the framed opening like a TV host commenting on the action. Our cats jump through this window and onto the counter sometimes before I swiftly guide them off. It all gets precarious when I set a steaming cup of green tea there or a bowl of pretzels.

We'd been living here less than two years. Already, we were keepers of the building's stories, passing down knowledge from prior tenants to new tenants. We'd learn the sounds of the voices of kids calling up and down the stairs, individual yet familiar parts of our routine, and then the family would move away, and we'd never see them again. Avoiding opening the envelope, I mulled all of this over while our cat Friday rubbed against my ankles and overheard voices call down the stairwell. A furry blue puppet danced around on the TV.

What was inside the envelope in my hands? It wasn't nothing. It was too thick to be nothing. But not thick enough to seem comprehensive. I closed my eyes, and an image of my grandfather's face appeared. I could see the crinkle lines around his eyes. I could see his haunted and lost expression while he stood in the unnamed ruins of a photo of the Pacific Theatre as a young man. Yes. I had his permission to find out more. Even if it was too much to comprehend. Or even if the letter discounted the whole book I had been writing.

I sighed.

I was ready. Ready for the truth.

The muscles of my stomach rubbed my worry into a sailor's knot. I slid my thumb under the flap of the envelope. The seal broke easily. I slid the papers into my hands and unfolded them. I swallowed. Here it goes.

"Dear Recipient:
Thank you for contacting the National Personnel Records Center. The record needed to answer your inquiry is not in our files," I read.

Oh. This again.
Another wall blocked my path.
I read on.

"If the record were here on July 12, 1973, it would have been in the area that suffered the most damage on that date and may have been destroyed."

A fire.
I imagined sparks catching a single page, and then maybe some microfiche or the corner of a manilla envelope. Maybe someone who came to the archives dropped a cigarette, or let the embers tumble into a stack of papers. Maybe that person watched the embers catch. The fabric pulling and growing. Red and orange peeling a brown edge from the pages and then eating them, blackening them into zeros, into dust and ash. Eating up words. Worlds.

What follows in the letter shocks me. "The fire destroyed the major portion of records of Army military personnel for the period of 1912 through 1959, and records of Air Force personnel with surnames Hubbard through Z for the period 1947 through 1963." S. The surname I was looking for was S.

I stood in my kitchen, listening to the high-pitched chatter of the TV, seeing father and daughter snuggled together on the couch watching the crayon-colored puppets run around and sing.

I was stunned by what I had read.

What this letter meant is that *any* family member inquiring about a relative's military service could receive no relevant information.

The fire of 1973, before the Watergate Scandal ended Nixon's second term early — which started just a month before the summer fire — ate through numbers, names, cities, weapons.

Ash, ash. Gone.

The fire erased all service records in the National Archives for WWI, WWII, the Korean War, and part of the Vietnam War.

The remaining pages in the packet of papers contained information about my grandfather's pay after the war, only for the year 1948. Also, the envelope contains a typed letter certifying that my grandfather was "re-rated" as a bombardier on August 25, 1948, when he flew one flight for two hours. And that was it. None of his service records during the Second World War were there.

I recently read in the *New York Times* that, according to historian Matthew Connelly, the mass *classification* of documents — the disappearance of historical information — is rooted in Cold War ideals.

Specifically, the origination of the Manhattan Project led to the handling of information that swiftly sweeps it into vaults, away from the general public forever.

I keep thinking about how The Pentagon Papers, leaked to the press in 1971 during Nixon's presidency, proved that the US Government intentionally misled the American public about the Vietnam War. How Nixon tried to sue the *New York Times* for publishing them. And how during Nixon's twilight as president — a few months before he resigned, the same month Nixon refused to hand over incriminating tapes, which the Senate then subpoenaed — a fire broke out in the National Personnel Records Center. A fire that ate through *all* of the military records indicating who did what in Vietnam. And in *all twentieth century wars the US fought*.

Was the fire a coincidence? A mind-blowingly destructive accident? I can't believe it was. But I can't prove it wasn't. No one can.

All the bombed cities, the tortured civilians, the sacrificed soldiers, the weapons technology, the orders obeyed, the orders misunderstood, the communications lost in thin air. Burned in the fire, gone. Anyone claiming to be part of anything couldn't completely prove their story. Nonfiction becomes fiction. Words become ghosts. Ghosts become shadows. What is missing might be all you have — the absence itself.

I ask myself more directly: *Had the records been burned on purpose?* Asking this question brings me to the edge of what I know and *how* I know. What would it mean for a nation to burn the records of the soldiers who enlisted or were drafted to fight for their nation, the story they believed about their nation? While the veterans' stories about their actions, what they might even tell, become pushed further and further away from the present with each generational death?

Sixteen to eighteen million files for military personnel burned to ash from the fire started at midnight on July 12, 1972. At the beginning of this book, I misguidedly thought the building would be in the Washington Metropolitan Area, but the National Personnel Records Center had been built in Saint Louis, Missouri. Even though firefighters arrived quickly, the fire erupted into walls of heat and smoke in the midwestern city. The fire burned until Friday, July 13. Firefighters had to wait a whole other day to enter. The air smelled acidic and thick.

Rumors of a cigarette are unproven. An electrical fire? Unproven.

There was a massive recovery effort for water-logged and molding documents. The National Personnel Records Center saved itself as a governmental institution. It appears to hold the records of veterans of US wars.

But again, I return to the letter I read in my galley kitchen on Friday the 13th: *The fire destroyed the major portion of records of Army military personnel for the period of 1912 through 1959, and records of Air Force personnel with surnames Hubbard through Z for the period 1947 through 1963.*

I think about how words redacted from FBI case files in the searchable records in their database look like bricks or obsidian stones.

Brick by brick, stone by stone, each redacted word, each absent word, becomes part of a wall.

Each wall becomes its own structure supporting the thing that cannot be named. But history — what we think we know about history

— is looming within these shadow structures. And inside, there are shadows of people, each with a heartbeat thrumming through a chest, believing their role within it or momentarily doubting it, but becoming part of the story all the same.

I think of buildings of hidden knowledge built from redactions. From absence. Bricks becoming towers.

I don't know who among the living can walk through these shadow buildings.

I don't know what it is like to stand inside of one of these rooms or what you can see out the window. I can guess, glimpse the shape sometimes of the city or catch a flicker that this shadow casts on a text I'm reading or a photo I accidentally possess.

Even though we rarely perceive the shadow running through some pages, the missing information appearing like a hole ripped in a fence, when we do, we still hold a cup to our lips and drink the water of our contemporary moment. The now is not then.

Except for when it is, the moment you glimpse and sense it. What happened. And how it has not gone away.

Acknowledgements

I am grateful to the editors of the following journals and magazines where these works first appeared, at times as earlier versions. All images are courtesy of the author.

AGNI: "Home"

Bennington Review: "Gone: An Elegy"

Brevity: "Backdrop: New Mexico" and "Boot"

Cherry Tree: "Body"

Cimarron Review: "Address"

Copper Nickel: "Front"

Gulf Coast: "Site: Snow in July"

Harriet: The Blog — Poetry Foundation: "Afterimage: Attempt at Description," "Stain," "Work," "Method," "Computer Punch Cards, Atomic Clouds, and Visual Language"

NELLE: "Bloom"

Poetry: "Afterimage (II)" and *"Afterimage (V)"*

River Teeth: "Boom: A Story of Erasure, Accident, and Exposure in the New Mexico Desert"

The Rumpus: "Periphery"

Tupelo Quarterly: "Afterimage (I)," "Afterimage (III)," "Afterimage (IV)," "Afterimage (VI)," "Afterimage (VII)," "Afterimage (VIII)," "Afterimage (XI)," "Afterimage (X)"

"Front" was awarded the 2015 *Copper Nickel* Editor's Prize in Prose.

Enormous gratitude to Unbound Edition Press, to Patrick Davis and Peter Campion for saying yes and believing in this book, and to Cory Firestine. I am indebted to the Café Royal NYC Cultural Foundation for awarding an earlier version of this manuscript a Literature Award, which supported the completion of this book. I'm also grateful to the Bethany Arts Community, the Doel Reed Center for the Arts in Taos, Ragdale, Yaddo, and the Women's International Study Center of Santa Fe for the residencies and fellowships that were invaluable to the writing and visual works in these pages. Thank you to Lynn Melnick, Leah Souffrant, Meg Lemke, Sarah Beth Childers, Shara McCallum, Daphny Maman, Jordan Young, Chet'la Sebree, Luis Urrea, Srikanth Reddy, Lauren Fath, Peter Buchanan, Renee Buchanan, Jennifer Hawe, Carol Moldaw, Doron Langberg, Gail Buono, Susan Steinberg, Tom March, Sven Birkerts, the New York Public Library's free resources for New Yorkers, the Palace of the Governors Photo Archives, and all of the editors of the journals who published essays from this book. Thank you to my colleagues at the Writing Institute at Sarah Lawrence College and the Provincetown Fine Arts Work Center's 24PearlStreet.

Thank you to Arik and our daughters, and to my parents. Thank you to my friends in Chicago, New Mexico, and NYC (you know who you are!) for listening, guiding, and being there. Gratitude to my teachers, my students, and my readers.

References

Godhead

US Department of Energy. "Nuclear Test Film — Trinity Shot." *Youtube,* uploaded by PublicResourceOrg, https://www.youtube.com/watch?v=oujy7AI1rac. Accessed April 24, 2023.

Prologue

Campbell, Richard H. *The Silverplate Bombers: A History and Registry of the Enola Gay and Other B-29's Configured to Carry Atomic Bombs.* Jefferson, North Carolina: McFarland & Company, Inc., 2005.

Haw, Jim. "Okinawa and the US military, post-1945." *Scientific American* [blog], June 19, 2013, https://blogs.scientificamerican.com/expeditions/okinawa-and-the-u-s-military-post-1945/. Accessed April 20, 2023.

Introduction

Mills, Tyler. *Hawk Parable.* University of Akron Press, 2019.

Sanger, David E. and William J. Broad. "Putin Declares a Nuclear Alert, and Biden Seeks De-escalation." *New York Times,* February 27, 2022, https://www.nytimes.com/2022/02/27/us/politics/putin-nuclear-alert-biden-deescalation.html. Accessed April 17, 2023.

Troianovski, Anton and Valerie Hopkins, Shashank Bengali, and David E. Sanger. "'Our Support Will Not Waver,' Biden Says After Putin Signals Sharper Break." *New York Times,* February 21, 2023, https://www.nytimes.com/live/2023/02/21/world/russia-biden-putin-ukraine-war#putin-and-biden-will-deliver-speeches-on-tuesday-here-is-what-to-know. Accessed April 17, 2023.

"New START Treaty." *US Department of State,* https://www.state.gov/new-start/. Accessed February 21, 2023.

Boom

"2017 Drinking Water Quality Report." lasvegasnm.gov. City of Las Vegas, New Mexico, 2017, lasvegasnm.gov/2017%20Drinking%20Water%20Quality%20Report.pdf. Accessed July 27, 2020.

"Area G Nuclear Waste Disposal Site." lasg.org. Los Alamos Study Group, September 30, 2019, https://www.lasg.org/waste/area-g.htm. Accessed July 27, 2020.

Barton, John. Personal Interview, May 20, 2018. "Best States for Education." *World Population Review,* August 8, 2019, worldpopulationreview.com/states/best-states-for-education/. Accessed July 27, 2020.

Donne, John. "Holy Sonnets: Batter my heart, three-person'd God." *Poetry Foundation,* 2023, https://www.poetryfoundation.org/poems/44106/holy-sonnets-batter-my-heart-three-persond-god. Accessed April 18, 2023.

"Facts, Figures." *Los Alamos National Laboratory,* ND, lanl.gov/about/facts-figures/index.php. Accessed July 27, 2020.

Kristensen, Hans M., and Matt Korda. "Status of World Nuclear Forces." *Federation of American Scientists,* May 2019, fas.org/issues/nuclear-weapons/status-world-nuclear-forces/. Accessed July 27, 2020.

Last, T.S. "Santa Fe Boom Came from Los Alamos Lab." *Albuquerque Journal,* January 11, 2018, https://www.abqjournal.com/1117974/santa-fe-boom-came-from-los-alamos-lab.html. Accessed July 27, 2020.

Machen, Judith, Ellen McGehee, and Dorothy Hoard. *Homesteading on the Pajarito* Plateau, 1887 — 1942, February 9, 2013, https://issuu.com/4cruz/docs/homesteaders/1. Accessed April 18, 2023.

Malone, Patrick. "Repeated Safety Lapses Hobble Los Alamos National Laboratory's Work on the Cores of Nuclear Warheads." *Science,* June 29, 2017, sciencemag.org/news/2017/06/near-disaster-federal-nuclear-weapons-laboratory-takes-hidden-toll-america-s-arsenal. July 27, 2020.

"MERTT: Radioactive Material Shipping Packages." FEMA: *Emergency Management Institute,* 20 June 2018, training.fema.gov/emiweb/is/is302/ss_mod05_sg.pdf. Accessed July 27, 2020.

Miller, Elizabeth. "Leaks from the Lab." *Santa Fe Reporter,* October 6, 2015, https://www.sfreporter.com/news/2015/10/06/leaks-from-the-lab/. Accessed December 2, 2020.

Monastersky, Richard. "First Atomic Blast Proposed as Start of Anthropocene." *Nature,* January 16, 2016, nature.com/news/first-atomic-blast-proposed-as-start-of-anthropocene-1.16739. Accessed July 27, 2020.

Moss, Rebecca. "LANL Blast Shakes up Santa Fe." *Santa Fe New Mexican,* January 11, 2018, santafenewmexican.com/news/local_news/lanl-blasts-shake-up-santa-fe/article_5ef77b76-f72c-11e7-bf98-cfd9f5077bed.html. Accessed July 27, 2020.

Nobel, Justin. "Atomic City." *Longreads*, September 2017, https://longreads.com/2017/09/05/atomic-city/. Accessed December 2, 2020.

"Nuclear Waste." *Los Alamos Study Group*, September 30, 2019, https://www.lasg.org/waste.htm. Accessed July 27, 2020.

Office of Environmental Management Technical Reports: A Bibliography, May 1999, https://books.google.com/books?id=d-1WWV6tfPwC&pg=PA113&lpg=PA113&d-q=Area+G+expansion+los+alamos+Tsankawi&source=bl&ots=-cirUJRIGGp&sig=ACfU3U1tKHIhm6-k2LXs4qZ7N8Dnd-vi18w&hl=en&sa=X&ved=2ahUKEwix-LWO3JLoAhWdlXIEH-f4rA9sQ6AEwAnoECAkQAQ#v=onepage&q&f=false. Accessed July 27, 2020.

Oswald, Mark. "LANL Docked $3.1 M for Shipping Plutonium via Commercial Air." *Albuquerque Journal*, January 19, 2018, abqjournal.com/1121661/los-alamos-docked-3-1-million-for-shipping-plutonium-via-commercial-air-cargo.html. Accessed July 27, 2020.

"Our History." *Los Alamos National Laboratory*, ND, lanl.gov/about/history-innovation/index.php. Accessed July 27, 2020.

Provost, Claire. "Atomic City, USA: How Once-Secret Los Alamos Became a Millionaire's Enclave." *Guardian*, November 1, 2016, theguardian.com/cities/2016/nov/01/atomic-city-los-alamos-se-cret-town-nuclear-millionaires. Accessed July 27, 2020.

"Radioactivity in Antiques." *United States Environmental Protection Agency*, Last updated August 27, 2019, epa.gov/radtown/radioac-tivity-antiques. Accessed July 27, 2020.

Rhodes, Richard. *The Making of the Atomic Bomb.* Simon & Schuster,
　　1987. —."War and Piece." Smithsonian, September 2019, 23–24.
Samenow, Jason. "Las Conchas Fire Near Los Alamos Largest in
　　New Mexico History." *Washington Post,* July 1, 2011, https://
　　www.washingtonpost.com/blogs/capital-weather-gang/post/
　　las-conchas-fire-near-los-alamos-largest-in-new-mexico-histo-
　　ry/2011/07/01/AGcNXptH_blog.html. Accessed July 27, 2020.
Siegel, Ethan. "Ask Ethan: How Can a Nuclear Bomb be Hotter than
　　the Center of Our Sun?" *Forbes,* March 28, 2020, https://www.
　　forbes.com/sites/startswithabang/2020/03/28/ask-ethan-
　　how-can-a-nuclear-bomb-be-hotter-than-the-center-of-our-
　　sun/?sh=4003dabc460b. Accessed December 2, 2020.
"Technical Areas." *Los Alamos National Laboratory,* ND,
　　wnr-web.lanl.gov/_assets/includes/all_tas.pdf PDF. Accessed
　　October 16, 2019. (Website unavailable as of July 27, 2020.)
　　Map can be found currently in the Department of Energy's
　　"Site-Wide Environmental Impact Statement for the Continued
　　Operation of the Los Alamos National Laboratory, Los Alamos,
　　NM, 1999, https://www.energy.gov/sites/prod/files/EIS-0238-
　　FEIS-01-1999.pdf. Accessed July 27, 2020.
Temperton, James. "'Now I Am Become Death, the Destroyer of
　　Worlds.' The Story of Oppenheimer's Infamous Quote." *Wired,*
　　August 9, 2017, wired.co.uk/article/manhattan-project-robert-
　　oppenheimer. Accessed July 27, 2020.
"Tsankawi." *Bandelier National Monument New Mexico.* National
　　Park Service, March 8, 2020, https://www.nps.gov/band/plan-
　　yourvisit/tsankawi.htm. Accessed July 27, 2020.

Tucker, Kathleen M. and Robert Alvarez. "Trinity: 'The Most Significant Hazard of the Manhattan Project.'" *Bulletin of the Atomic Scientists,* July 15, 2019, thebulletin.org/2019/07/trinity-the-most-significant-hazard-of-the-entire-manhattan-project/. Accessed July 27, 2020.

"US Regulators to Investigate After Los Alamos Lab Improperly Shipped Nuclear Material." *CBS News,* June 23, 2017, https://www.cbsnews.com/news/los-alamos-shipped-nuclear-material-by-plane-authorities-say/. Accessed July 27, 2020.

Wellerstein, Alex. "The Demon Core and the Strange Death of Louis Slotin." *The New Yorker,* May 21, 2016, https://www.newyorker.com/tech/annals-of-technology/demon-core-the-strange-death-of-louis-slotin. Accessed July 27, 2020.

Gadget

United States Air Force. "1945 — Project Tower — Trinity A-Bomb Camera — Color — HD — Footage." YouTube, uploaded by Historical Videos HD, https://www.youtube.com/watch?v=W-jrElz7dh3U. Accessed April 26, 2023.

Periphery

Anderson, Benedict. *Imagined Communities.* Verso, 2006.

Anzaldúa, Gloria. *Borderlands / La Frontera.* 2nd. Ed. San Francisco: Aunt Lute Books, 1987).

Frosch, Dan. "Decades After Nuclear Test, US Studies Cancer Fallout." *Wall Street Journal,* September 15, 2014, wsj.com/articles/decades-after-nuclear-test-u-s-studies-cancer-fallout-1410802085. Accessed May 19, 2017.

"Hiroshima and Nagasaki Missions — Planes & Crews." *Atomic Heritage Foundation,* last modified 2016, atomicheritage.org/history/ hiroshima-and-nagasaki-missions-planes-crews. Accessed May 19, 2017.

"Kenneth Bainbridge." *Atomic Heritage Foundation,* last modified 2016, atomicheritage.org/profile/kenneth-bainbridge. Accessed May 19, 2017.

Leaver-Yap, Mason. "Comprehensive Horrors and Technological Consequences: Bruce Connor and Leslie Thornton." *Walker Art Center,* April 8, 2016, blogs.walkerart.org/film-video/2016/04/08/bruce-conner-leslie-thornton-bikini-atoll/. Accessed May 19, 2017.

Lewis, Renee. "Bikinians evacuated 'for good of mankind' endure lengthy nuclear fallout." *Aljazeera America,* July 28, 2015, amer-ica.aljazeera.com/articles/2015/7/28/bikini-nuclear-test-survi-vors-demand-compensation.html. Accessed May 19, 2017.

Muir, Douglas M. "Trust Territory of the Pacific." *Encyclopedia.com* (from *Dictionary of American History*), 2003, encyclopedia. com/doc/1G2-3401804289.html. Accessed May 19, 2017.

"Operating Hours & Seasons (White Sands)." *National Parks Service,* n.d., nps.gov/whsa/planyourvisit/hours.htm. Accessed May 19, 2017.

"Operation Crossroads." *Atomic Heritage Foundation,* July 1, 2014, atomicheritage.org/history/operation-crossroads. Accessed May 19, 2017.

"A Short History of White Sands National Monument." *National Parks Service,* n.d., nps.gov/whsa/learn/historyculture/short-history-of-white-sands-national-monument.htm. Accessed May 19, 2017.

Sontag, Susan. *Regarding the Pain of Others.* Picador, 2004.

Stevens, Wallace. "Thirteen Ways of Looking at a Blackbird." *Poetry Foundation,* last modified 2017, poetryfoundation.org/poems-and-poets/poems/detail/45236. Accessed May 19, 2017.

Sumner, Thomas. "Bikini Atoll radiation levels remain alarmingly high." *Science News,* June 6, 2016, sciencenews.org/article/bikini-atoll-radiation-levels-remain-alarmingly-high. Accessed May 19, 2017.

"Trinity Site Open House is Saturday." *Las Cruces Sun-News,* September 28, 2016, lcsun-news.com/story/news/2016/09/28/trinity-site-open-house-saturday/91248316/. Accessed May 19, 2017.

"Trinity Test Eyewitnesses." *Atomic Heritage Foundation,* last modified 2016, atomicheritage.org/key-documents/trinity-test-eyewitnesses. Accessed May 19, 2017.

US Army. *White Sands Missile Range Customer Handbook,* September 26, 2012. wsmr.army.mil/pdf/RCH2012FinalOPSECApproved26September2012.pdf. Accessed May 19, 2017.

US Department of Energy Nevada Operations Office. *United States Nuclear Tests July 1945 through September 1992,* December 2000, digital.library.unt.edu/ark:/67531/metadc721128/m2/1/high_res_d/769260.pdf. PDF. Accessed May 19, 2017.

"White Sands." *National Park Service,* n.d., nps.gov/whsa/index.htm. Accessed May 19, 2017.

Gone: An Elegy

"Public Health Response to Severe Influenza" (formerly "Public Health
Response to a Nuclear Detonation." *Centers for Disease Control
and Prevention,* Last updated January 26, 2018, https://www.
cdc.gov/cdcgrandrounds/archives/2018/January2018.htm.
Accessed January 17, 2018. ("Public Health Response"). I later
found the original webinar advertised on a different site, the
National Alliance for Radiation Readiness: http://www.radiation-
ready.org/event/public-health-response-to-a-nuclear-detona-
tion-webinar/ Accessed October 19, 2019.

Afterimage (V)

Atomic Energy Commission. "Declassified Nuclear Test Film #12
(Operation Ivy, Parts 1 and 2,"1952). *Youtube,* uploaded by
talkingsticktv, https://www.youtube.com/watch?v=7E3y63gK-
GwA. Accessed April 26, 2023.

Ghost

Atomic Energy Commission. "Leslie Groves Speaking to the Officers
Regarding the Atom Bomb." *National Archives,* 1945, https://
iowaculture.gov/history/education/educator-resources/prima-
ry-source-sets/world-war-ii/general-leslie-groves. Accessed
July 31, 2022.

EPA. *Abandoned Uranium Mines on and Near Navajo Nation,*
March 30, 2016, https://www.epa.gov/sites/default/
files/2016-06/sfd1602325_allaums_0.png. Accessed
May 6, 2022.

Klauk, Erin. "Human Health Impacts on the Navajo Nation from
Uranium Mining." *Science Education Resource Center,* Carleton
College, May 5, 2022, https://serc.carleton.edu/11000. Accessed
May 6, 2022.

Luokkala, Sonia. "Abandoned Uranium Mines Plague Navajo Nation."
Earth Island Journal, May 5, 2015, https://www.earthisland.org/
journal/index.php/articles/entry/abandoned_uranium_mines_
plague_navajo_nation/. Accessed May 6, 2022.

"Monument Valley." *National Park Reservations,* 2022,
https://www.nationalparkreservations.com/article/monument-
valley/. Accessed May 6, 2022.

Perez-Sullivan, Margot. "EPA Awards Contracts Worth up to $220
million to Three Companies for Cleanup at Navajo Nation Area
Abandoned Uranium Mines." *EP: United States Environmental
Protection Agency,* February 11, 2021, https://www.epa.gov/
newsreleases/epa-awards-contracts-worth-220-million-three-
companies-cleanup-navajo-nation-area. Accessed May 6, 2022.

Tabuchi, Hiroko. "Uranium Miners Pushed Hard for a Comeback. They
Got Their Wish." *New York Times,* January 13, 2018, https://
www.nytimes.com/2018/01/13/climate/trump-uranium-bears-
ears.html. Accessed May 6, 2022.

"Uranium Mill Tailings." *United States Nuclear Regulatory
Commission,* March 12, 2020, https://www.nrc.gov/waste/
mill-tailings.html. Accessed May 6, 2022.

Address

"Bombings of Hiroshima and Nagasaki." *Atomic Heritage Foundation,*
June 5. 2014, https://www.atomicheritage.org/history/bomb-
ings-hiroshima-and-nagasaki-1945#:~:text=The%20deci-
sion%20to%20use%20the,until%20the%20country%20sur-
rendered%20unconditionally. Accessed May 6, 2022.

Davis, Richard. "Spaatz." *Air Force Magazine,* December 1, 2020,
https://www.airforcemag.com/article/1200spaatz/. Accessed
May 6, 2022.

Feis, Herbert. Japan Subdued: *The Atomic Bomb and the End of
the War in the Pacific.* Princeton University Press, 1961,
pp. 184 – 185.

"Hiroshima and Nagasaki: 75th Anniversary of Atomic Bombings."
BBC, August 9, 2020, https://www.bbc.com/news/in-pic-
tures-53648572. Accessed May 6, 2022.

"Order to Drop the Bomb: Handy to Spaatz, National Archives (July
25, 1945)." *US Department of Energy,* 2013, https://www.osti.
gov/opennet/manhattan-project-history/Resources/order_drop.
htm & https://www.osti.gov/opennet/manhattan-project-history/
publications/droporder.pdf. Accessed May 6, 2022.

Statue

Ahmed-Ullah, Noreen S. "Study Says O'Hare Emissions Hike Cancer
Risks." *Chicago Tribune,* August 27, 2000, https://www.chicag-
otribune.com/news/ct-xpm-2000-08-28-0008280214-story.
html. Accessed May 6, 2022.

Chen, Desiree. "O'Hare's Pollution a Cloud of Controversy." *Chicago Tribune,* December 22, 1996, https://www.chicagotribune.com/news/ct-xpm-1996-12-22-9612220198-story.html. Accessed May 6, 2022.

"Des Plaines." *Collins Dictionary,* 2022, https://www.collinsdictionary.com/us/dictionary/english/des-plaines. Accessed May 6, 2022.

"First Atomic Bomb Dropped on Japan; Missile is equal to to 20,000 Tons of TNT; Truman Warns Foe of a 'Rain of Ruin.'" (headline) *New York Times,* August 7, 1945, https://archive.nytimes.com/www.nytimes.com/learning/general/onthisday/big/0806.html. Accessed May 6, 2022.

Cards and Clouds

"1 March 1954 — Castle Bravo." *Comprehensive Nuclear-Test-Ban-Treaty Organization,* https://www.ctbto.org/specials/testing-times/1-march-1954-castle-bravo, Accessed May 6, 2022.

Chen, Agnus. "In the Event of a Nuclear Blast, Don't Condition Your Hair." *NPR.org,* August 15, 2017, npr.org/sections/health-shots/2017/08/15/543647878/in-the-event-of-a-nuclear-blast-don-t-condition-your-hair. Accessed May 6, 2022.

"Marshall Islands." *Atomic Heritage Foundation,* 2019, atomicheritage.org/location/marshall-islands. Accessed May 6, 2022.

Wang, Amy B. and Brittany Lyte. "'BALLISTIC MISSILE THREAT
    INBOUND TO HAWAII,' the Alert Screamed. It was a False
    Alarm." *Washington Post,* January 13, 2018, washingtonpost.
    com/news/post-nation/wp/2018/01/13/hawaii-residents-get-bal-
    listic-missile-threat-messages/. Accessed October 16, 2019.

Trinity

"About — White Sands Missile Range." *US Army,*
    https://home.army.mil/wsmr/index.php/about#:~:text=WS-
    MR%20encompasses%203%2C421%20square%20miles,-
    DoD%20airspace%20in%20the%20country. Accessed
    May 6, 2022.

"Eighth Air Force History." *8th Air Force* / J-GSOC, n.d.,
    https://www.8af.af.mil/About-Us/Fact-Sheets/Display/Arti-
    cle/333794/eighth-air-force history/#:~:text=For%20this%20
    reason%2C%20Eighth%20Air,compiled%20an%20impres-
    sive%20war%20record. Accessed May 6, 2022.

Fisher, Max. "As Russia Digs in, What's the Risk of Nuclear War? 'It's
    Not Zero.'" *New York Times,* March 16, 2022, https://www.
    nytimes.com/2022/03/16/world/europe/ukraine-russia-nucle-
    ar-war.html. Accessed May 6, 2022.

"Owner Refuses to Leave Ranch on Missile Range." *New York Times,*
    October 15, 1982, https://www.nytimes.com/1982/10/15/us/
    owner-refuses-to-leave-ranch-on-missile-range.html. Accessed
    May 6, 2022.

"Twentieth Air Force Fact Sheet." *20th Air Force*, October 2021, https://www.20af.af.mil/About-Us/Fact-Sheets/Display/Article/825610/twentieth-air-force-fact-sheet/. Accessed May 6, 2022.

United States. US House of Representatives, *Research and Development for Defense Hearings Before the Committee on Science and Astronautics,* Eighty-seventh Congress, first sess. Washington, 1961.

Site: Snow in July

Segarra, Curtis. "77 years later, New Mexicans still hope for recognition of atomic fallout." *KRQE News,* September 13, 2022, https://www.krqe.com/news/politics-government/77-years-later-new-mexicans-still-hope-for-recognition-of-atomic-fallout/. Accessed March 13, 2023.

Leede, Katherine and Maggie O'Brien. "'Downwind' of Trinity: Remembering the First Victims of the Atom Bomb." *NTI: Nuclear Threat Initiative,* July 15, 2021, https://www.nti.org/atomic-pulse/downwind-of-trinity-remembering-the-first-victims-of-the-atomicbomb/#:~:text=In%20New%20Mexico%2C%20where%20ranchers,downwind%20of%20the%20nuclear%20blast. Accessed October 26, 2022.

Rhodes, Richard. *The Making of the Atomic Bomb.* Simon and Schuster, 1986.

Bloom

The Bible. New King James Version, Oxford UP, 1998.

Craig, Paul A. *The Killing Zone: How and Why Pilots Die.* New York: McGraw Hill, 2001.

Dickinson, Emily. *The Complete Poems of Emily Dickinson.* Ed. Thomas H. Johnson. Cambridge, MA: The Belknap Press of Harvard University Press, 1983.

Coda. Fire

"The 1973 Fire, National Personnel Records Center." *National Archives,* 2023, https://www.archives.gov/personnel-records-center/fire-1973. Accessed April 20, 2023.

Crossland, April. Official Letter. National Personnel Records Center. January 6, 2023.

Weiner, Tim. "When the Government Goes Top Secret, Who Can Write Its History?" *New York Times,* February 8, 2023, https://www.nytimes.com/2023/02/08/books/review/the-declassification-engine-matthew-connelly.html. Accessed April 20, 2023.

About the Author

Tyler Mills (she/her) is the author of *City Scattered* (Snowbound Chapbook Award, Tupelo Press 2022), *Hawk Parable* (Akron Poetry Prize, University of Akron Press 2019), *Tongue Lyre* (Crab Orchard Series in Poetry First Book Award, Southern Illinois University Press 2013), *Low Budget Movie* (co-authored with Kendra DeColo, Diode Editions 2021), and *The Bomb Cloud*. She teaches for Sarah Lawrence College's Writing Institute and lives in Brooklyn, NY.

About the Type and Paper

Designed by Malou Verlomme of the Monotype Studio, Macklin is an elegant, high-contrast typeface. It has been designed purposely for more emotional appeal.

The concept for Macklin began with research on historical material from Britain and Europe dating to the beginning of the 19th century, specifically the work of Vincent Figgins. Verlomme pays respect to Figgins's work with Macklin, but pushes the family to a more contemporary place.

This book is printed on natural Rolland Enviro Book stock. The paper is 100 percent post-consumer sustainable fiber content and is FSC-certified.

The Bomb Cloud was designed by Eleanor Safe and Joseph Floresca.

Unbound Edition Press champions honest, original voices.
Committed to the power of writers who explore and illuminate
the contemporary human condition, we publish collections of poetry,
short fiction, and essays. Our publisher and editorial team aim
to identify, develop, and defend authors who create thoughtfully
challenging work which may not find a home with mainstream
publishers. We are guided by a mission to respect and elevate
emerging, under-appreciated, and marginalized authors, with
a strong commitment to advancing LGBTQ+ and BIPOC voices.
We are honored to make meaningful contributions to the literary arts
by publishing their work.

unboundedition.com